Somewhere Along the Way

by
Wilmoth Foreman

Dedicated to

husband Jesse,

who took time away from his real job
to format, organize, and shape these writings
into a book

and to

friend Robert Stone,

who, for all these years,
critiqued all these columns.

Table of Contents

Critters

Perspectives

Food

Great Outdoors

War

Recent History

Music

Keeping Up Appearances

Predicaments

Sporting Chance

Et Cetera

Meditations

Critters

Three's a Crowd for Coffee in the Swing

Dog: "What does that newcomer have that I don't have?
All these years I've loved you…"

In our household one long-established tradition, weather permitting, is that the resident dog joins me in the swing for an early morning cup of coffee.

Dog is not as young as she once was. To negotiate this swing thing, she has to get a running start, charge full-speed ahead, and take a flying leap to land by my side. Hence, it's important to quickly drink the coffee down to a level that won't slosh.

Once we are settled, the next few moments proceed in a calm and reflective manner. Or did, till complications purred onto the scene last spring.

In the fervent hope that Dog can't read, I herein admit that, in my heart of hearts, I am ever a cat person. No way does this lessen my devotion to Dog. It just means that, since Sylvie Dee's demise, there is a missing that won't go away.

To be sure that missing remains intact, Dog has gleefully chased any newcomer cats who amble up, hoping to reside on the premises. That strategy worked — for Dog, better than for me — till a neighborhood cat, in response to Dog's attempt to chase her, sat down.

I hurried to the store for a bag of cat chow.

Now, first thing each morning, she sits on my back step, half a nose from the door, staring at that huge wooden vertical slab that temporarily bars her from Breakfast # Who-Knows-How-Many?

Simple enough, you say. Just open the door, throw the food out, and get on with it.

But remember. There's a 99% chance that, somewhere on the patio, an equally expectant dog also waits. So the deal is: arm myself with two helpings of dry food, set my coffee where I can reach it once breakfasts are served, and crack the door an inch or so.

The one thing I've willfully disobeyed is Cat's request to dine indoors. So next comes a clumsy weaving-cat-versus-garden clogs ballet before the door can be closed with both me and Cat on the outside.

With a prim "Good morning," she continues: "I thoroughly agree with you that I am the most wonderful cat in the world and am aware that you hugely hope I'll abandon he who raised me and come live exclusively with you bearing that in mind it would please me no end which I'm aware is your aim in life if your alarm could be set so that this breakfast could be served nearer 5:00 than 6:00 thereby not forcing me to eat fast in order to be on time for the one across the street which by the way is a better brand of food but …it's been hours since breakfast at my house and I am down to skin and bones, so…"

Kerplunk. Mid-novella, Cat jumps up to the shelf that's too high for Dog to reach and paces with such persistence, it takes careful aim to pour the food where she doesn't knock it off.

Once food is available, her soliloquy is instantly replaced by crunching.

After all that hecticity, emptying the dog food container half a patio away is relatively easy. But I must harden my heart to THE look that telegraphs: "Dog food? Again? After all the times I've begged for the other?" (Gazing wistfully at the cat eating the coveted cat food…) "What does that newcomer have that I don't have? All these years I've loved you…"

At last. Lukewarm coffee, a gently swaying swing…and Dog, abandoning her boring breakfast to galumph toward me.

Not only is this quality swing time long established; it's closely guarded. So Cat's early efforts to horn in were quickly, and literally, squashed.

One morning when Cat's spin on our relationship was evolving from skittish to cautious, she decided to join me in the swing. Just as she meowed, "this actually almost feels like a comfort zone," 35 pounds of self-propelled dog seemingly fell out of the sky and flattened her. By the time the fur got sorted, Cat was on the ground while Dog waggingly kissed my chin.

This happened twice before Cat caught on.

Now, with two in the swing and one in or under a nearby tree, we watch the world wake up, we three.

Clueless Millicent's Past, Present, and Iffy Future

Mama Mussel fashioned a decoy fish,
floated the 'bait' just above her shell, and waited.

Millicent Mussel spends her days ooched (rhymes with mooched) down in the river bottom of Duck River's shoals (shallow places). The thickest part of her bilateral oval shape stays buried in the sand; her shell's smaller end points up into the water.

Millie keeps her shell partially open so she can filter food out of the water that flows past. When some macho mussel upstream adds his calling card to the water and fertilizes Millie's eggs, she incubates them in her shell until they become baby mussels. Lots of baby mussels.

This triggers a big-time case of cabin — uh, shell — fever. Millie isn't much of a traveler. Nor were her mother and grandmother or all those ancestors back to the ice age and beyond. But in some previous era, one mama mussel who'd had a really bad day trapped in that shell with all those unruly offspring vowed, "I gotta get these kids outta here!"

Then as now, transportation options in the water world mostly had fins. Given her sedentary nature and lack of limbs, Mama Mussel couldn't chase down a fish. So the best solution to her 'close quarters' problem was to lure a fish to her, let her offspring hitch rides, and wave as they left on their way to lives of their own.

So using what was available — herself — Mama Mussel fashioned a decoy fish, floated the 'bait' just above her shell, and waited. Sure enough, a real fish came to investigate. While it nosed around, checking out the fake one, Mama Mussel, stifling sighs of relief, shooed her wee babes onto the fish's gills.

You know how word spreads about a new "Mother's Day Out" program! From that day forward, Mama Mussel had a waiting list for her Intermediate Fish Designs class. Her generation passed the skill on, and making fish decoys was soon built into the mussels' genetic heritage.

Meanwhile, back to the babies. They clung onto their host fish's gills for three or four weeks. When mature enough to fend for themselves, they 'jumped ship' at some shoal their fish swam over, and their substitute 18-wheeler swam away, none the worse for wear.

So on to the 21st century, wherein Millicent is at her shoal, her posterior ooched in for a life that, if she escapes her role in the food chain, may last 70 to 80 years. There she sits, up to her underarms in sand, relieved that the kids are finally on their own; clueless to the fact that her species' miraculous centuries-spanning survival could be dead-ended.

She's oblivious, period, for Millie has no brain. She is just a mass of muscle with a penchant for survival. But fake fish is her sole strategy.

Will her plan, pitted against humans' tendency to destroy whatever is in their path toward 'prosperity,' suffice as a survival technique? Millicent doesn't even realize that, if those fish her offspring hitch rides on don't survive, neither will she.

It's called the balance of nature, Millie. And so far, it's alive and well in Duck River. Seven of our continent's ten richest rivers are in Tennessee. Of those, the Duck — rich in aquatic species because glaciers didn't alter its ecosystem — is second in North America only to Clinch River (east of here) as a natural history museum of aquatic life for this temperate zone.

Surely, wreaking havoc on this delicate balancing act is not the answer to long-term survival for Millie or her two-legged neighbors. There has to be a better route to prosperity than tunnel-vision environmental destruction.

The Naming and Taming of a Wounded Feathered Friend

When the engine started,
it began clacking its beak at a fast, rhythmic pace
that sounded like castanets.

This is how we met: On the drive back from taking a babysitter home, something was flapping around in the middle of the dirt road. A wide-eyed screech owl glared back at the headlights' beam. Stilled by our presence, it sat with its right wing stretched out, the left one folded tight against its body.

"It won't live long out here," I told Walt and Ellen, who were equally wide-eyed in the back seat. "I'll put it in the front floorboard."

There was a hand towel in the car. Towel in hand, I circled the owl. It moved to always face me. When I stooped to pick it up, it crow-hopped away, hissing. But my second try was successful.

Except for the protruding broken wing, the trembling body was no bigger than my fist. In the front floorboard, the owl made a few feeble attempts to fly, then scrunched as far back as possible into the far corner under the dashboard. When the engine started, it began clacking its beak at a fast, rhythmic pace that sounded like castanets.

One of the kids said, "It sure is ornery." So Ornery Owl had a name before we got home.

The owl's first night's lodging was a cat carrying case. Before getting deposited there, Ornery endured a few moments' petting. "You're gonna get tamed," I warned. He didn't blink.

Breakfast was unseasoned scrambled eggs and raw hamburger, served on a plastic top next to Ornery's water bowl. He was so hungry, he started eating with us watching. Every bite was attacked ferociously enough to rip up a mouse or some other critter-meal. The plastic top danced up and down on the flat cage floor and eggs bounced everywhere.

For a permanent home, a men's-wear store gave us a big box that hats came in. We added a tree limb and new-fallen leaves. Ornery promptly hid in the leaves and didn't come out till we got tired of watching and left.

A sturdy window-screen covering was supposed to keep Ornery in. But it didn't. It took several searches to find him scrunched in a dark corner of a bookcase — a space seemingly too small for a mouse, much less an owl. Weights on the screen cut off his escape route.

By the third day, Ornery sat on his tree limb. Several times a day, 'we' talked while I held him. Rather, I talked and he listened. One day, rather than picking him up and holding him firmly in both hands, I held my finger out beside his tree limb. He stepped onto it like he'd been perching there all his life. It took about three seconds for his grip to totally numb my finger; industrial strength gloves got added to the shopping list.

When I held Ornery at arm's length on his finger perch, he'd watch me with unblinking eyes. Slowly, I'd turn my hand so that his body faced 180 degrees in the opposite direction. But his head — and that unblinking stare — would still be facing me.

During one of our long, arms'-length conversations, I must've hit on a subject dear to his heart. He suddenly walked up my arm and settled into a nose-to-beak proximity. It was the era when our society was just becoming aware of drug-use needle marks. The trail of puncture wounds left in Ornery's wake necessitated wearing long sleeves, both in public and during future owl-human chats.

Ornery became tame enough that I dared take him to our son's kindergarten class, where he performed his entire repertoire — perching, neck swivels, staring, arm-climbing — with nary a hitch.

Twice a day, we had 'flying therapy' in the living room. Ornery would take off; barely get up in the air; then, a foot or so away, crash land. These sessions were kept to five minutes, hopefully to strengthen rather than further injure the broken wing.

But the night did come that, since owl and humans all seemed to be enjoying flight practice so thoroughly, we overdid. The next morning, Ornery was a lifeless wad of feathers in his hatbox home.

A friend who knows these things recently told me we should have fed him whole mice; that he needed the calcium in the bones to rebuild the crippled wing.

Some lessons are learned too late.

Tribute to an Ordinary, though Quirky, Cat

The morning I found her dead in her bed,
I returned to the living room to get her body
and it wasn't there.

The night before I found Sylvester Dweezel Foreman not breathing in her cat bed, I'd decided to catch up on long distance phone calls. Sylvie came into the room and rubbed against my leg. I ignored her, so she launched into her 'notice me or else' strategy — rattling a sack; threatening to unravel computer wires; pouncing on un-pounceables.

Even when she worried the hall closet's sliding door open, it didn't distract me from chatting. But once she was inside the closet, her scratching was so frantic, I had to intervene before she shredded an entire spring wardrobe.

Next, she galloped from one end of the house to the other. "This cat has reverted to kittenhood," I commented across a thousand miles.

By the time I got off the phone and settled into my chair in the living room, she was curled up in her bed nearby. And was still there, motionless, the next morning.

"So that's what last night's rampage was about!" I thought. "Her innards were giving her fits. Terminal ones."

The morning I found her dead in her bed, I returned to the living room to get her body and it wasn't there. I'd been wrong in presuming Sylvie wasn't breathing

She lived another month. Her daily routine became: an hour outdoors about 9:00 a.m. followed by bed rest; an afternoon hour outdoors; a visit about 9:00 p.m. with Pansey dog, who was always waiting by the back door.

After each outing, she'd rattle the storm door to get back in.

The day I decided it was 'time,' Sylvie asked to go outside before 7:00 a.m. Twelve hours later, I had to go find her. The same thing happened the next day. I decided she had overheard my conversation with the veterinarian about euthanization and was deliberately disappearing during office hours.

The next day, Sylvie was too weak to go outside, but we honored her decision to die at home.

Her failing health had begun with dry cat food coming up faster than it went down. So we changed to soft serve food. Sylvie seemed better, but not well. By the time the two of us went to the vet, I expected only one would come back.

At least temporarily, tests ruled out the fear that she needed to be euthanized. A daily dab of laxative cream was prescribed. For good measure, mineral oil was to be added to her food.

The oil proved to be a better lube job than the more expensive spread. But it took only two servings for her to recognize the additive. One sniff of the laced morsels and she'd launch into a meowed "I can't believe you're trying this again" lecture and refuse to eat.

By the morning I found her curled up and immobile — really not breathing — she was skin and bone. Jesse was napping in his recliner nearby and there was no hurry, so I tiptoed away to weep and reminisce.

How old in human years is a cat that's going on 18? She had borne and outlived two kittens; been spayed; survived years of intimidation until alpha cat Sweetface moved to Nashville with Kate; overcome her terror of, then become fast friends with, our dog Pansey.

Her favorite food was tuna juice. Yet, if offered a chunk of the tuna meat, her reaction was, "They're trying to poison me!"

She loved big bosomed women. Given half a chance to get in their laps, she'd endlessly rub against them, no matter how red their faces in a room full of people.

Her other favorite place was the back yard. That's where we buried her.

Yesterday I noticed a wad of black fur on the kitchen floor and was about to pick it up when I realized, "Sylvie's been dead for weeks!"

The 'fur' was a spider that got swatted.

Fur-free floors, tuna juice down the drain, opening the storm door to find it was the wind, not the cat, rattling it. These are among the reminders.

Sylvie wasn't a miraculous cat, give or take her ability to adapt and survive. But she was a good cat whose joyous kitten soul bubbled to the top often during her long adulthood.

A characteristic — and a cat — worth remembering.

A Furry Testimonial for Recycled Pets

"She's sweet," said one of the workers…
"We're not here to get a dog," I answered.

Was it just six years ago that we made that trip to the recycling center out the Santa Fe Pike? We passed the side road where the Maury County Animal Shelter is located. Kate had recently mentioned the possibility of doing volunteer work there during her summer break from school. "Remind me to stop on the way back so you can check it out," I casually said.

I didn't need reminding.

We walked in to muted bedlam; it crescendoed whenever someone opened the door to where the residents were caged. A receptionist eventually emerged and asked, "Would you like to see the animals?" Well, why not?

Some of the cats were too adorable to look at; our aging matriarch already had her paws full making life miserable for the household's newest feline. I had to bodily wrestle Kate away from all those "I'm the one for you" purrs and meows.

The dogs were in long, roomy cages. Lots of cages, lots of dogs. As if on cue, they began to vie for our attention with barks, wags, raring up on the bars, eye contact. They acted like humans trying to get chosen by the host of some crazy game show. One teenaged black chow plastered himself sideways against the cage door so firmly that his fur came through the bars, and the eye he rolled toward us threatened to follow. Even in that silly state, he was gorgeous. And noisy.

Down two cages to the right was a dog that was more my type — big enough to not dig under our fence, but not big enough to jump it. Vague lineage. Bushy. Not as frantic as some. Yet, when we sidled its way, it began to leap and yap.

The cage between those two seemed empty. But toward the back sat a fairly large black and white dog, quietly observing the commotion. Its 'been there, done that' look implied a refusal to get its hopes up for yet another disappointment. I tried to coax it to the front of the cage. It just smiled and stayed put.

"She's sweet," said one of the workers who noticed which dog I was eyeing. "Would you like for me to get her out so you can visit with her?"

"We're not here to get a dog," I answered.

"There's a room down the hall where people can get acquainted with the animals." Evidently, she hadn't heard my disclaimer.

When we got into the room and the collar came off, the dog licked my hand as if to say, "excuse me a moment," went to a corner of the room, and had a highly successful bathroom bout. "That's a good sign," said the attendant. "Some of them will mess up their cages. The polite ones wait."

Kate's version: "Mama, she wasn't playing hard-to-get. She just had her legs crossed."

Beauty was not this dog's selling point. She was sway-back, had a crooked (broken?) tail, and a cut on the nose that looked like a wart. But her impeccable manners and good nature won our hearts.

When we said we'd like to adopt that dog, the attendant said, "Oh, good! We've already extended the deadline for putting her to sleep, hoping someone would come for her."

On the way home, Kate added, "When you stopped there, we both knew we'd come home with a dog."

It wasn't until we'd signed the papers that we were given the name and phone number of the person who'd brought Daisy Mae (Jesse named her) to the shelter. Daisy had come all the way from Pulaski! After living with this eager-to-please creature for two weeks, I had to know why she'd been dumped.

"We bought this place to raise ponies on," said her former owner. "Blackie (the name they'd given her) came with the farm...was living in a barn. Some workers who were here before us said she'd been there quite a while."

I asked why they got rid of her. "We really liked her," she said. "But we already had two big dogs, and a baby. When the ponies started foaling, that was just too much to manage."

"But why bring her over here?"

"We did a lot of checking around. We felt that the Maury shelter was very caring and tried their best to place adoptable animals." She added, "We really wanted Blackie to find a home."

Our family is fortunate that Daisy Mae Dog landed in our household. Her physical scars from years as a stray are now minimized by happy eyes and lots of wagging. People who see her for the first time usually say, "What a beautiful dog!"

Which she is.

Perspectives

A Mostly Unplumbed Perspective on Black History

And my, the laughter in that kitchen! It all seemed so natural.
But eventually the girl realized that maybe it wasn't.

With the Middle East in crisis and Mother Nature on the rampage, the arrival of Black History Month has been so downplayed, I looked it up to be sure. And yes, since 1976, February has been Black History Month in the United States and Canada.

The idea was born in 1926 when African-American Carter G. Woodson proclaimed a Negro History Week. Its goal was to educate the American people about African-Americans' cultural background and reputable achievements.

To a casual observer in the 21st century, the month's focus on our (historically recent) struggle for equal rights overshadows Woodson's intended 'culture and achievements' agenda.

Perhaps this is as it should be. The dramatic struggle for equality is well documented in word and film. Fire hoses, snarling faces, expletives, vicious murders — like scenes from the Holocaust — urge us to watch for clues and not go there again. But mostly missing, except in fiction, is the silent mass of Caucasian do-nothings — those who, even as they became aware of injustices, kept quiet.

This inner conflict is masterfully depicted in Mark Twain's much-beleaguered novel, *The Adventures of Huckleberry Finn*. The title character ricochets between his growing friendship with Jim, a Negro runaway, and Huck's gut feeling that, by respecting this man, he is betraying all he's ever known. No way could the depth of this inner struggle be plumbed without Huck's use of the hated N-word to bolster his tenuous hold on what he's been taught.

Less dramatic than 19th century ambivalence and 20th century mob scenes is the perspective of a little white girl who, beginning some 71 years ago, grew up in the segregated South in a town known as Columbia, Tennessee.

Her parents, like everyone else's, were emerging from the upheaval of

World War II. Her family, like many others, was short on cash but high on values and patriotism. It took quite a while for her to notice that one thing about her family was different from those at church and school. Her mother's best friend was a Negro.

Neither of the women drove. So her mama and Aunt Sadie's visits were limited to times when Sadie's grown son dropped her off at their house.

Though the girl's family were not huggers, when Aunt Sadie landed, there was no escape from getting hugged. A big, laughing, disappearing in it hug. Often followed by the gift of a silver dollar.

After the furor, they settled in, usually around the table. And my, the laughter in that kitchen! It all seemed so natural. But eventually the girl realized that maybe it wasn't.

"A long time ago, I needed some help with something," the mom said when the girl asked how the friendship began. "Sadie was recommended and I hired her. Don't know how we had the money…After that, we just kept visiting."

A remembering look came over her. "At that time, I was sewing for the public…" She chuckled, then told of the time Aunt Sadie was there when a snippy customer tried on a dress the mother had made. "These darts aren't even," the woman complained. "Fix them. I'll be back Monday."

When the woman left, the mother examined the dress, then told Sadie she didn't know how to improve on the darts. "It's not the darts, Honey," Sadie said. "It's her. You hang that dress in the closet and don't touch it. Come Monday, she'll say you did fine repair work." Which is exactly what happened.

On days when the girl stayed home sick, she discovered that, the minute their houseful of kids left for school, her mother phoned Aunt Sadie. Every weekday, that short chat was a jumpstart necessity relished by both women.

In that era, any storebought item anyone could possibly want was available within a couple of blocks of Columbia's courthouse. When the girl got big enough to go downtown with her friends, she'd occasionally see Aunt Sadie's handsome, impeccably dressed son Hank talking with someone half a block away. The minute Hank saw the girls approaching, he'd discreetly move so that his back was to them; the girl could walk by without having to speak.

It made her mad. She'd walk around to face him, then say loud and clear, "Hello, Hank! How's your mother?" He'd respond with a tip of his hat, a dip of his shoulders and, "Just fine. So good of you to ask."

"Why wouldn't I want to speak to him?" she'd inwardly fume as she caught up to the other girls. "He's a college graduate. A teacher!"

Maybe she was already in Whitthorne Junior High that day when, while shopping, she needed a restroom. Not many downtown stores had public restrooms, but she knew one that did.

The sign on the bathroom door was one she'd seen all her life: Whites Only. At that moment, for the first time it hit home. What if Aunt Sadie was shopping and needed a bathroom? Would she have to go home? The realization lasted a small moment. Only to resurface in bothersome ways.

(to be continued)

A Mostly Unplumbed Perspective on Black History, Part 2

His mother laughed and said,
"That ball field belongs to the white kids during school hours.
But when they go home, it's ours."

The girl's first awareness of how different life in the same town was for whites and blacks revolved around her mother's best friend, Aunt Sadie, who was a Negro.

When the girl was a child, Sadie's son Hank would bring his mom to the girl's house for visits. His car was always a late model; spit-shined; a thing of beauty.

She was too young — or too indifferent to that sort of thing — to compare it to her family's vehicle, whose every fiber testified that it was a workhorse for a rowdy family of six.

Something she did notice was that Hank always, always, like his car, looked spit-shined. All he'd need to be ready for church was a coat and tie.

Why would a grown man be that dressed up mid-week!?!

She was way past grown before wondering if these outward manifestations were ways to visualize a dignity that was denied elsewhere. White-owned car dealerships and men's clothing stores didn't mind taking money earned by a teacher in one of the county's Negro schools. And that money sure couldn't be spent in restaurants. Or dropped into collection plates in white churches.

Aunt Sadie and Hank's family lived together in a large house near one of the town's all-white schools. When the girl became a teenager and got her driver's license, she'd occasionally chauffeur her mom over there for a visit.

One sunny Saturday when the weather was too perfect to waste, the girl, her mom, Aunt Sadie and Sadie's daughter-in-law sat outside in yard chairs, within sight and sound of a noisy baseball game on the school grounds.

Sadie's grandson was one of the players. His mother laughed and said, "That ball field belongs to the white kids during school hours. But when they go home, it's ours."

In typical "I try my best, but..." mom-mode, she added, "And no matter how much I nag, Son just will not remember to wear a hat. By the end of summer, he'll be black as midnight."

"Whattt?" thought the girl. It amazed her to realize that colored people (at that time, this was the respectful term to use), like her own race, were preoccupied with skin tone. Was it possible that, while whites ruined their skin tanning themselves on beaches, the coloreds were trying to turn pale?

The girl's mom subscribed to a lot of magazines — Ladies' Home Journal, Family Circle, Woman's Day to name a few. The girl often read articles in them, especially those about subscribers' poignant life experiences. One day she was reading a young mother's story about the fun her toddler had playing with a delightful child they'd met on the playground of a nearby park.

Obviously, the story was leading toward some traumatic outcome. Turns out, to keep her daughter from being ostracized by her own race, the mother quit taking her child to that playground when the two children arrived at an age where, in that community, it was not acceptable for whites and blacks to be seen together.

The writer secretly hoped that, by the time her girl was grown, the two playmates could renew their friendship. "I'd rather my daughter's friends be colored," she concluded, "than colorless."

Back to the 'little girl' from Columbia, Tennessee. She reached college age; a campus became her world. There was one TV in her entire dorm, in the lobby, but nobody watched it. She wasn't interested enough in world events to buy a newspaper. So the first she knew of regional unrest was via a concerned call from her mom.

"Sit-ins?" The girl didn't understand the concept, and hadn't a clue that they were happening just blocks from her campus cocoon. "I never go there," she assured her mom. And that was that.

Till, during summer break back in Columbia after a ball game, she was part of a group that went to a fast-food restaurant to celebrate their team's win. A black family came in and sat at the counter. With exaggerated movements, many of the salt-of-the-earth whites she had come with immediately got up and left. She was surprised and embarrassed by their actions, but said nothing.

When busloads of freedom riders came south, she vaguely wondered what business they had here. Finally, finally, media coverage with pictures of hate-filled faces spewing hate-words woke her. In her mind, she chose sides — the same one the freedom riders came down on — but continued doing nothing. Integration happened despite the protesters against it, perhaps equally despite the inaction of her ilk.

Years after Aunt Sadie's death, through political and civic elbow-rubbing, the girl, now grown, discovered that Hank's entire adult life was filled not only with family, but with good friends whose social and community lives were rich and rewarding.

Within their realm, they had elected to not be bothered by segregation. Just as she had elected to ignore its existence.

Preparing For and Surviving
an Estate Sale

It's the unexpected that gets you in the gut.

Our family recently experienced what many others will sooner or later be faced with: a houseful — really full — of things that can no longer be there.

We, like many others, decided to have a sale.

First off we learned that, when choosing a name for the event, 'estate sale' has nothing to do with the definition of 'estate.' What 'estate' says to potential customers is that, rather than moving outgrown clothes and toys, this sale is clearing out generations of accumulations. It may or may not be a Mecca for collectors and antique dealers.

Next we learned that a sale of this sort is like a wedding. No matter how near or far off it is on the calendar, until it's over, it consumes you.

Sorting is the name of the sale game. What-to-keep constantly looms as a big decision. For me, living nearby was a huge advantage. I'd drag something home, think about it overnight, and drag it back to the sale site the next day. A room in our house that's now piled up with boxes, pictures, etc. testifies that the 'dragging-back' wasn't always the case.

One friend commented, "It must be so hard putting price tags on all that priceless stuff, even, or maybe especially, the junk."

Yes and no. You steel yourself and get on with the business at hand, much of which consists of pulling stuff you didn't even know was there out of dark corners until the spiders think they're in the middle of World War III.

There are actually milestones that become reasons to rejoice — a jewelry box emptied, a room cleared; a who-gets-what resolved to everyone's satisfaction.

It's the unexpected that gets you in the gut:

-counting cups and, due to the lack thereof, envisioning Maw healthy, happily working at her dish-breaking whirlwind pace in her favorite place, the kitchen;

-finding, under a pile of papers, a stuffed toy that zooms you back to when its owner loved it unconditionally and was 110% scrutable;

-needing a light, automatically plugging it in and, for the first time ever, wondering, "Why did he always turn this one on and off with the plug instead of the switch?"

Of all the sale lessons learned, the most basic was: Since you don't know diddly, get help from those who understand how this should work, start to finish.

Our #1 Organizer's philosophy was, "Presentation, presentation, presentation." This advice translated into hours of washing linens, dishes, cookware, even furniture and appliances.

We had a foolproof Master Plan for the day of the sale. It was rich in details such as not admitting eager beavers a moment before the stated opening hour; who was to monitor which areas; what prices were negotiable. Dream on.

The strangest things sell. Wonderfully wonderful items large and small languished unnoticed while a young lady struggled to drag a dilapidated record player to the checkout table. In line ahead of her, a hulk of a guy clutched his find – a rusty 'antique' cheese grater – to his chest.

As to pricing, it's damned if you do, damned if you don't. Each time a knowledgeable antique dealer or collector snapped something up and paid the asking price without a whimper, the realization was, "They're gonna make a killing on that."

When a valuable item got passed by – especially the big ones that would have to be lugged elsewhere – the wonder was, "Might that have moved if the price had been better?"

Perhaps the most flustering lesson of the sale was, "This is the age of dickering." No longer do most customers pay what's posted and leave. "Will you take…?" was the norm. Except for aunts who insisted on paying full marked price for what we would have preferred they took for free.

The bottom line is, what if some dealer sells a piano bench for 10 times the price we got for it? Not a single spider in our garage can play 'Chopsticks' from having inhabited that bench. And, because it and myriad other stashed-aways are now being appreciated elsewhere, we can see our way clear to disposing of what's left.

Hence, our estate sale can be summed up as 'all's well that ends well.' It has helped us along the path toward a final time to unplug that light and walk away.

How One Person Kicked the Habit

"I can do this," she said, and threw her cigarettes in the garbage.
Only to, after most stores were closed, shell out highway robbery prices
for 'just this one pack' at a convenience store.

It began in college. Outside the cafeteria, a company rep was handing out sample packets of cigarettes, four to a pack. She and her roommate each took one. Back in their dorm, they had to borrow matches to light up. Then snuffed out half-smoked cigs to save them for the next day.

By the end of the week they'd squandered one whole pack, and the roommate had lost interest. So the next four were hers, all hers. With rationing, they ought to last for eight days.

They didn't. The natural solution was to buy more. And begin her journey down the well-worn path toward addiction.

Onward to marry a smoker and eventually have a family — kids who, when they got big enough, would occasionally hide her cigarettes. But they weren't very good at it. She always found them.

The years passed with little if any thought of quitting. To run out of milk was a minor problem, not worth a trip to the stores, all of which closed at 6:00. Except for that one convenience store with its sky-high prices.

But if the stash of cigarettes became dangerously low, she'd pile the kids into the car by 5:45. Maybe, to give the trip to the grocery legitimacy, buy some milk along with the pack of Benson & Hedges menthol.

After nearly fourteen years of addiction, she was up to over a pack a day. And the cost was rising. A carton was nearly $20; vending machines had gone up to 75¢ per pack. Her habit was getting to be a major expense.

Yet, despite money matters and escalating public/medical opinion that smoking might be hazardous to your health, she continued to smoke.

Two juxtaposed things did crack the invisible protective wall she'd built around her habit. One was a pain — a searing pain that, if she took a deep breath, shot parallel to her spine down the right side of her back.

"I'd better check it out," she told herself and made an appointment for x-rays. Which showed nothing amiss. But she knew better.

The other: an illustrated magazine article. Not only did it spell out her habit's dangers. It pictured a lung before and after smoking. The first picture was a blackened mess. The second, taken just a year after quitting, was a healthy red. The article assured smokers that, even if their habit was long-term, smoke-free lungs could heal themselves.

It also described in lay terms how addiction works. "Your body builds up an army to resist what's bad for it," said the article. "When the bad thing (like smoking) happens again and again, that army gets habited to surging forth to fight that enemy. It gets so used to rallying for the cause, it will show up even if the enemy doesn't."

"I can do this," she said, and threw her cigarettes in the garbage. Only to, after most stores were closed, shell out highway robbery prices for 'just this one pack' at a convenience store.

Again and again she'd buy a pack; smoke a few, spaced at long intervals; throw the pack away. She and the convenience store clerk were on first-name basis. "This isn't working," she finally admitted. And the shooting pain was still there. She either had to quit or never again breathe deep.

Patches hadn't been invented; hypnosis was out of the question. She came up with one more option: She'd keep cigarettes onsite. And diet simultaneously, so as not to substitute food for smokes.

Wherever she went, the cigarettes went. One pack stayed in the car, one in her purse. When she prepared meals, a pack was within reach on the counter. At times when, as described in the magazine, her "inner army" charged forth to fight the enemy, she'd hold tight to kitchen cabinet edges to keep her hands from grabbing a cigarette.

The plan worked; she quit smoking. A year or so later, her husband also quit.

Months after the smell of cigarette smoke no longer permeated their house, it still hit her full force whenever she opened her clothes closet. And for several years she said, "The minute I'm pronounced terminally ill, I'm gonna light up."

That vow, too, has passed. Seldom does a wafting tendril of cigarette smoke cause her to sigh and inhale deeply.

But when it does, breathing deep is free of sharp pain.

One Book's Beginnings and Early Life

In the dining hall to the left, to the right, and across the table were students eagerly sharing plot plans for novels.

Did you ever wonder how books get born? Please say yes. The only one I know about for sure is the one I wrote. Here's its story:

In the late '90's, our son Walt, via a fellowship, was working on a Masters degree in writing at Johns Hopkins. One day I casually mentioned to him that I might some day go back to school in that same field.

He cautioned, "Mama, I thought I was pretty liberal. But…" As gently as possible, he let me know that 'his' writing program and many others nationwide would shock me silly.

I'd already taken every possible local course, then had my feelings hurt when a North Carolina school turned me down. So I dismissed the whole thing.

Months later, I got a packet from Walt about a Vermont College program titled Writing for Children and Young Adults. In it was a note saying, "This may be more your speed." The program spanned two years, was pricey, involved five trips to Vermont, and was self-contained, so no other graduate credits could be factored in.

North Carolina didn't want me; Vermont probably wouldn't either. Why not apply?

I got accepted.

The first few minutes on that northern campus in below-zero January temperatures, it became apparent that I was in tall cotton. The faculty's collection of impressive credentials was topped only by their friendliness.

In the dining hall to the left, to the right, and across the table were students eagerly sharing plot plans for novels. I dared not open my mouth, partly because my southern accent drew attention. But also because I had no ambition to pen a novel. I just wanted to learn to write better.

Toward that end, first semester advisor Norma Fox Mazer stressed that, to write fiction, one must turn loose of what really happened. "Sometimes you have to go beyond facts to get to the truth," said she.

Second semester, as I stretched to invent stories, advisor Carolyn Coman observed, "You write so well about your past. Why won't you let yourself go there?" So I went there, drawing heavily on the newfound freedom Norma had given me to make stuff up.

Near the end of our time together, Carolyn urged me to pick a third semester advisor who would help wrestle the stories triggered by real life into a cohesive whole. Fantasy and historical fiction writer Susan Fletcher filled that bill.

Fourth semester, Carolyn asked to see what progress we'd made, so I obliged her with a copy of the manuscript.

A month later, back in Tennessee, the phone rang. The caller introduced himself as Carolyn's editor/publisher. Unknown to me, she had asked him to read my writings. Talk about a Cinderella moment! One sentence he said is forever engraved in my heart and brain: "I have read your manuscript and I love it and I want to publish it."

At the time the contract was signed, the novel was less than half written. A grueling cycle of writing, waiting, rewriting and line editing spanned 18 months before the book appeared in stores and libraries.

Somewhere along that way, 'my' editor asked if there was anything about the whole process that was bothering me. I replied, "People keep asking me what age I'm writing this for. I don't know."

His expletive-deleted answer was, "You are writing it for readers."

After *Summer of the Skunks* became a done deed, I learned that writing a book is just the beginning. Promoting it is a biggie with its own huge area of know-how, most of which is learned by trial and error when it's too late.

But, hey! Despite my lack of promotional skills, 'Skunks' is in its second printing. I try to help it out here and there with readings and signings

If you are a reader, I hope to someday see you in the audience!

Food

A Fowl Recipe That'll Drive You to Drink

"Buying beer is more complicated than I thought," I say.
"That's not beer," he replies.

This whole outing is the fault of a gift I gave husband Jesse for Christmas. I'd heard him talk about a unique chicken-cooking gizmo that you poured beer into, then propped a chicken carcass on top. The result was supposed to be ultra tender and tasty. In a last minute gift-search tizzy, I'd seen one and bought it.

"I'll never use this," he said when he opened the package.

Well! If he wouldn't, I would… Which is why I'm standing in the beer aisle on Sunday, wondering if Blue Laws are still in effect. There are no padlocks, so maybe not.

"This stuff is pricey," I realize. One that's on sale is mostly gone. The lonesome six-pack that's left is so far back on the top shelf of the cooler, I couldn't reach it if I crawled in. No one tall comes by, so I re-check the offerings and pick a familiar name that's reachable. Its bottles are clear glass and it'll set me back over $6.00. But I need beer.

Farther down the aisle, I notice some brown bottles for nearly half the price of what's in my buggy. The brown looks more beer-ish, so I pick one of those six-packs, try to find where the one I no longer want came from, give up and cram it into the cooler any old where.

At the checkout lane the young cashier says, "I need to see identification."

"At my age? You're kidding."

"No. They passed a law last summer."

As I show him my driver's license, I say, "I'll have to find someone young to drink this stuff. I'm buying it to cook a chicken with."

At home with my purchases, I hurried to put away groceries, leaving the beer on the counter. The chicken in its future is already waiting in the refrigerator, and is next on the to-do list. Jesse saunters in.

"Buying beer is more complicated than I thought," I say.

"That's not beer," he replies.

"It's brown."

"Looks like near beer to me." He reads the label out loud. "Contains less than 0.5% alcohol by volume."

"So what does that have to do with anything? The chicken doesn't care."

Buying the beer isn't this recipe's only complication. The gizmo's directions say "225 to 250 degrees for about 45 minutes per pound" and "plug top of chicken with an onion." That first directive involves math and planning ahead. And who'd have thought that convincing an onion to not dive into the beer would morph into an engineering feat?

Ensconced on its pedestal, that chicken is funny-looking. I open the oven door to show Jesse. "A fowl-mouth stand-up comic?" he asks.

The baking takes even longer than predicted due to frequent oven door openings to peer in for a good laugh. Yet, as promised, the bird is tender and tasty. So food-wise, the new gadget works.

But regarding its success as a trend-setting gift? Next year, it's back to handkerchiefs and terrible ties for you-know-who.

Some Pointers about Poke

When to pick it? I prefer spring, while snakes
are sleepy and poison ivy is still dormant.

The phone call is overdue this year. It goes something like this: "You want some poke sallet? Better come on out. It's everywhere, but I'm about to bushhog it." Every year, I ask, "Is it where the cows won't get me?"

Armed with a paring knife and a couple of sacks, I walk my brother's fence row looking for what the dictionary calls pokeweed. By the time I get home, what seemed like a reasonable harvest while picking it has multiplied to much more than I want to clean and cook. But I clean and cook it anyway.

Here's how: wash the greens in salt water to kill any bugs. If the stems are big, peel them and cut them into chunks. Boil stems and leaves in a copious amount of water till they look thoroughly discouraged — 20 to 30 minutes. Using a colander, pour off the water; it's supposed to be poisonous, but I've never tested that theory. Squeeze the water out of that piddling green glob your original tons of poke shrunk to.

Chop and smush what's left and put it in a skillet with hot bacon grease. Stir it about 'til it's hot, add raw eggs — how many is a by guess/by golly decision — and scramble the whole she-bang. Serve with cornbread, green onions, and maybe cheese grits, if the intent is regional fare. Fatback optional.

Poke sallet's use as a vegetable is probably more southern than its growth is. A few weeks ago, I visited Youngstown, Ohio, with a friend. There was an enviable stand of poke in the back yard of the house where her son lives. Since Youngstown is just minutes away from the Pennsylvania border, it's safe to surmise that pokeweed (I feel traitorous using the term 'weed') grows as far north as Pennsylvania. It's rampant in St. Louis where my sister lives. She never picks it; too many chemicals on the yards in her neighborhood.

Where to find poke locally? It grows wherever it can...in fence rows, along roadsides, in newly disrupted dirt such as mined or bulldozed areas, around buildings and tree trunks. It appears in the spring about the time asparagus peeks out...early enough to identify itself with the season, but late enough to avoid heavy frosts. It 'pokes' out of the ground with leaves snug around the stalk. The hotter the weather, the more enthused the leaves get. A mid-summer stalk may sport leaves over a foot long.

How to identify poke? Beats me. Once, Jesse eyed a fresh-picked batch suspiciously. "How do you know that's all poke?" he asked. When "I just do" and "You don't have to eat it" proved unsatisfactory answers, I asked, "How do you know a Leica camera when you see one?" That made no sense, but was as good an answer as, "It's genetic."

When to pick it? I prefer spring, while snakes are sleepy and poison ivy is still dormant. But some people harvest the tender new growth of mature plants all summer. The purple berries it has in the fall are poisonous, but are good for 'dying' spelled the hue/color way.

Those who are hooked will go to some lengths to assuage their taste for poke. Years ago, when The Daily Herald offices were downtown on Garden Street, the paper's 80-something widowed co-owner was a great devotee of poke sallet. Mr. Walter Hastings let this be known through his writings. Predictably, people would show up at The Herald with 'a mess of poke' for him. He'd carry it by the sack-full to Oldham's Restaurant, a meat-and-three favorite with the downtown crowd. With winks and whisperings, he'd plot with the staff. Then, he'd go back to the office and invite a chosen few to the restaurant for a meal featuring his readers' poke offering. The new advertising director, young Jesse Foreman, would be one of the chosen.

Here's a favorite third-hand poke story: Columbia Power had just installed a chain link fence around their Pickens Lane site. The person responsible for security got reports that someone was sometimes seen inside the fence when the place was locked up, both early morning and after hours. There was no sign of forced entry, and the gate was always properly locked after the sightings. The mystery was solved when a company official explained, "Mrs. So-and-So asked for a key so she could come in and pick poke sallet."

I like to serve this family favorite to those who've never tried it. The resulting comments vary from "interesting" to "pretty good" to "no, thanks." What I'm shooting for is an unqualified "Wow!"

Gobbling Up a Turkey-less Thanksgiving Dinner

The jello globs out onto the platter and slumps there in a sagging heap that in no way resembles the vision I had of a wonderfully festive side dish.

Thanksgiving Day. Both daughters are helping in the kitchen, and the appointed hour for our midday feast is fast approaching. So is a daughter. She needs something out of the drawer I'm blocking.

"This just proves my theory," I tell her, "that if two people are in a kitchen at the same time, one of them is always where the other one needs to be."

The reason we keep tripping over each other is that we're trying to salvage a truly strange menu by adding a few last-minute dishes. This year's non-traditional choices border on weird because Kate has become vegan, which is one degree beyond vegetarian. She not only does not eat meat; she doesn't eat dairy products, eggs, or anything cooked with ingredients that are animal byproducts.

This not only gives Tom Turkey a reprieve. It knocks out a host of bought soups; baked goods with eggs and/or milk in them; and veggies seasoned with meat or cheese. Thumb through a lifetime collection of recipes with those limits in mind, and see how many qualify.

I've made a jello/cranberry concoction that's sure to pass the vegan test. I dunk the mold in warm water. "Do you want me to flip that jello mold?" Ellen asks.

"Yes, I've been worrying about that moment." I hand it to her and stand back. SHPLUNK! The jello globs out onto the platter and slumps there in a sagging heap that in no way resembles the vision I had of a wonderfully festive side dish.

"The last time I made this," I say, "I wrote on the menu to allow a full day for it to gel. This time, I gave it two days."

Ellen eyes the jiggly mass. "Does it have pineapple in it?"

"Yes."

"That's your problem. Pineapple has an enzyme that keeps jello from congealing."

Kate comes by for a viewing. "I can't eat that," she says. Before I can ask why, Ellen says, "Because it's made from cow hooves."

In an effort to have something special for the vegan one, Ellen is preparing roasted Brussels sprouts with a complicated non-cream creamy mustard sauce. The oven needs to be 400 degrees for the sprouts, but only 300 for heating up various other dishes. The compromise is an oven made dizzy by temperature adjustments up and down.

My zeal at loading the dishwasher isn't helping the mustard sauce. "Did you get my whisk again?" Ellen asks. For the second time, I retrieve the utensil, asking, "So you want me to not load the whisk?"

"Yes. I do. Want you to not load the whisk."

"What about the big fork?"

"It was a 'poke the Brussels sprouts' fork. They're done at last. You can have it."

"Did you remember to cook the country ham?" Kate asks. A close call! That last-minute slice of ham and deviled eggs are designated to save the day for our meat-and-three man of the house.

When we gather, I announce to family and vegetarian guest, "Although I cooked it, I am not responsible for the rice." It's an 'old faithful' recipe substituting vegetable broth for beef stock. The result, rather than the usual brown, is orange.

The eggs are a hit with our vegetarian friend and the vegan one has ample choices. As for the Brussels sprouts? Erratic oven temps have given them a tough hide heretofore unknown to the sprout kingdom. We take Ellen at her word that after a trial run in her kitchen with her ground rules, they were tender and juicy.

Despite this minor tragedy, a good time and plenty of food is had by all. After the dishes are done and no one is around, I look at the Jello box list of ingredients. Not a word about hooves; just 'gelatin.' Who'd have thought of that term as a euphemism?

Hankering for Some Very Vegetable Soup

Peer at the spice rack. If anything sounds like it would add pizzazz, consider it.

For those of us who inherited it, the homemade-vegetable-soup gene kicks in about this time of year. Those who missed out on this gene should not despair. With or without inborn knowledge, there are almost as many routes to success in this culinary endeavor as there are kitchens. Here are a couple:

Ingredients can begin assembling themselves long before 'soup's on.' Liquids from canned vegetables, instead of going down the drain, can be collected bit by bit in a really big freezer bag. At soup time, these make a tasty, semi-nutritious stock (the liquid base that everything else is cooked in). Likewise, leftover tomato slices, peeled and frozen, accumulate nicely to include as a soup ingredient.

For Soup Day, absolute musts to have on hand are potatoes, carrots, celery, onions. Choose a cooking utensil that's bigger than you think it needs to be and that won't stick. Now, have at it.

Step one: Hold that frozen hunk of vegetable juices under hot water until it will slide out of the bag. Heck, life is short; get the scissors and cut that bag off of there. Start melting that giant ice cube conglomerate over medium heat while you chop, chop, chop.

Begin with what will take longest to cook — potatoes, carrots, celery. Don't throw away those leafy tops. Chop 'em up and pitch 'em in. Even if you don't love it elsewhere, herein okra adds uumph. If it's added early enough to disintegrate, it won't be noticed.

Got garlic? Chop it up and put it in, along with an onion. Stir before the potatoes and carrots glom on to the bottom of the pan. Search the freezer in hopes of finding corn, peas and such. Add a couple of handfuls of each. Next, rummage through those canned goods. If you find green beans, dump them in, liquid and all.

Stir. It's probably time to turn the heat down from purposeful to meditative.

For heartiness, you may want to throw in the towel — scratch that; the devil made me do it. Instead, throw in a handful of rice, or some pasta. Bowties are cute. Whatever. Now, it's time to add those frozen tomatoes. Canned ones work just as well.

Squash doesn't add much taste-wise, but it looks nice. At the other end of that spectrum, realize that cabbage, broccoli, and peppers hot or mild all affect the flavor big time. Your soup; your choice.

Peer at the spice rack. If anything sounds like it would add pizzazz, consider it. But don't get too adventurous; you've gone to too much trouble to mess it up.

Want cornbread with your soup? Turn the oven to 400 degrees, heat oil in an iron skillet, and pour into it a concoction of, for a small skillet, no more than a half cup of self-rising corn meal, some oil, an egg, and enough buttermilk.

For the "tell me again what this button on the stove does" generation, the good news is, you can probably get delicious 'homemade' results by buying bags of frozen chopped veggies, dumping them into a good-sized pot of hot water with salt, pepper, an all-purpose seasoning, and maybe a bouillon cube or two. Or bought broth. Crackers are acceptable in lieu of cornbread.

But for the old school, there's something intrinsically noble and satisfying about all that chopping. Whichever route you choose, don't forget to stir.

Great Outdoors

Signs of Spring from Around the Country

I wanted to rush outside and shout,
"Go back south! Winter isn't over yet!"

Here are some responses to an all-points bulletin inviting folk to share 'signs of spring' from their regions:

OREGON: Buying the first asparagus and strawberries of the season (shipped in from California), putting on a coat to plant pansies, and watching rain drench the camellias.

NEW MEXICO: The Santa Fe River runs like mad through downtown with the snow that melts from the Sangre de Cristo Mountains. The Fish and Wildlife Dept. stocks it with trout and you see families all along the river with their rods, bait, and picnics, enjoying a weekend of free fishing.

MAINE: Yesterday, two bluebirds visited our bird feeder. I wanted to rush outside and shout "Go back South! Winter isn't over yet!"

MICHIGAN: News reports of Coast Guard rescuers pulling ice fishermen off ice floes that are heading for Niagara Falls; motorcycles, and people bundled up with scarves and ear muffs, driving top-down convertibles.

MASSACHUSETTS: Little girls begin playing jump rope in the street; kids carrying baseball or softball gloves waiting for the bus. And bikes begin to appear.

THE CATSKILLS, NEW YORK: Waking up to mourning dove cooing — you know, the mating/courting sounds the male makes. The arrival of wood ducks on the pond is a very clear sign, as is the increased activity of the pileated woodpeckers. House spiders wake up and crawl over everything — shoes, blankets, toes. One can find wild asparagus, morels, and fiddlehead ferns.

MAINE: Maple sugaring, and then, sugar on snow! Maple syrup is boiled to a certain temperature, then drizzled over a dish of CLEAN packed snow. It becomes like taffy, which you pick off the snow with a fork and devour, yum yum, until you get sick. It is usually served with doughnuts and pickles (to cut the sweetness).

FLORIDA: It's the sycamore trees. They are the only trees in Florida that really tell us what time of year it is. In the summer the leaves are bright green and as soft as satin. When fall comes, the leaves turn yellow and stiffen to brown. Then the winter winds blow the branches clean. The skeleton of the tree waits for spring, then soft green buds poke through toward the sun. We are just at the edge of spring now. I can't wait for the sycamore to be full again.

SYRACUSE, NEW YORK: Handwritten "See you in the spring" and "Closed for the season" signs come down from places like Vicky's Ice Cream Stand and Hafner's Nursery (which has been closed since the last Christmas tree was sold). The green and white striped awning goes up over the windows of my favorite restaurant, and the plastic fisherman who sits in a rowboat on its roof dons his yellow raincoat and hat. (At Christmas time, he has a Santa suit; at Easter, bunny ears.)

MONTANA: Spring? What's that? It's been below zero off and on for two weeks and counting...

Gardening: It's All About Grit, Grime, and Grace

*Once the seeds and plant food and basic equipment
follow you home, the real work begins...*

This time of year, this column is going to be about digging up a lot of dirt. Not the tabloid 'celeb secrets' variety, but good clean garden dirt. Which, by the way, is not all that easy to dig.

Having gardened since childhood, I heartily recommend going there and doing that. I can even offer advice to newcomers. After all, I've made every gardening goof in the book, and am still at it.

First of all, forget the romanticized notion that growing flowers and veggies is a leisure pastime. The truth is: from start to finish, gardening is work. As a species, plants are demanding. If they're going to feed you — or in the case of flowers, nourish your soul — you'd better return the favor. From preparing the soil before they get in it to extra helpings of nutrients during growth to fending off ever-encroaching weeds, you need to be there for them.

And remember. Some of your leafy charges will be heavy drinkers. They're root-bound, so don't expect them to raid the refrigerator for their beverage of choice. The solution has legs and a watering can, and is spelled g-a-r-d-e-n-e-r.

Help is available to make these demands easier to cope with. Which brings us to the myth that gardening saves money. The lyrics to an old song says, "...it's not raining rain, you know. It's raining violets." Ain't gonna happen. You want violets, you go to the violet store. And while you're there, buy violet food and a trowel to plant and cultivate them with. And watch out! En route to the checkout lane, those color picture packets on the seed rack will leap willy-nilly into your shopping cart.

Once the seeds and plant food and basic equipment follow you home, the real work begins...closely followed by labor pains and visions of work-saving devices you breezed past that first trip down the gardening aisles.

Most of those helps are spelled e-x-p-e-n-s-i-v-e. I recently read a book by William Alexander expounding on his long history of growing things. He does not use equipment with loud engines such as tillers and power-driven mowers because he prefers serenity while gardening. Despite his reliance on labor-intensive tools and the sweat of his brow, Alexander estimates his cost per harvested veggie in the book's title — *The $64 Tomato.*

As for me and my garden, we have no qualms about energy beyond my own. For nearly 25 years, my tiller Matilda and I serenely — and noisily — gardened together. After her get up and go went kaput, so did my garden. Now, as a smaller and less capable tiller attempts to fill Matilda's tire prints, it has already surpassed her in price and noise.

Oops. Wasn't I out to convince non-gardeners that they ought to plant things? I'd better change tactics. Suddenly my keyboard is tongue-tied. Exactly what are the good parts to gardening?

Watching stuff grow and change; being not only outdoors, but being a part of what outdoors is. Amid the weeds and failures, occasionally creating a seed-catalog-cover visual; harvesting what you helped make happen.

Does it count that it's impossible to plant and tend anything without witnessing miracles? What a wonderment when rock-hard beans sprout and asparagus emerges from spidery crowns that look like they crawled out of Stephen King's monster-filled brain.

As one sage noted, "I feel closer to God in my garden than anywhere else." A garden — a good place to be. Amen.

Raucous Love Songs and Doggy Snack Attacks

As to the "There's something good about everything" maxim,
Pansey dog has been in snack heaven.

Ah, what's not to love about cicadas?

Everything. Their red beady eyes; their over-the-top raucous 'love song' sung endlessly; the way they crash into you or fly into the car each time a door opens.

The noxious noise began in early May. By mid-month, as the sun rose, their racket amplified into a steady stream of loud that didn't let up till dark. One wonders if the mating call really does sound romantic to the female of the species. Or if a more realistic scenario is: "Anything to get him to shut up..."

By early June, the wee beasties were dying in droves. Even their deaths were overdone — plummeting from tree limbs like lead balloons; final flights ending in a kamikaze crash landing; upside down swirling-dervish 'dances' on sidewalks, patio, solid rock.

As to the "There's something good about everything" maxim, Pansey dog has been in snack heaven. She spurns heaps and piles of dead cicadas for fresh-meat ones that are still barely kicking. When a snack attack strikes, nose to the ground she scans every inch of an area, like one of those metal detectors used by treasure-seekers.

Her best shopping takes place under my favorite (and only) weeping willow. From the time the cicadas appeared, its tender branches have been their favorite hangout. When the locusts were at their loudest, walking beneath that tree was akin sound-wise to entering a sonic blast zone.

Which explains this news item: An East Tennessee man called police to complain about heavy machinery that was ceaselessly disturbing the peace in his area. "I've driven all over the place, but can't locate it," he told them. Turns out, the offending noise was cicadas.

After about five minutes outdoors, it's been possible to tune the rascals out. So peaceful co-existence has been our lot...up to a point. That point being, the moment I noticed entire lengths of the willow's strands turning crisp. How do you declare war on millions of locusts? There seemed no option but to hope for recovery and wait it out.

This past Monday was auspicious. Not till Pansey passed up her dog food breakfast to graze for cicadas did I realize that the only songs in the morning air came from birds. An occasional locust rasp did mix in with the chirps. But even those were half-hearted, staccato, short-lived.

In our own back yard, midday locust sounds, though still part of the outdoor background music, are no longer all-encompassing. Hopefully, our month-long cicada onslaught is about to be past tense. Good riddance.

Doomsday for Doofus

*The top-of-the-line brand is expensive. But the clerk who demonstrated
how to bait the cheaper model got his hand caught.*

This is the story of Doofus. And of tipsy sunflowers. And of once-leafy squash plants' determined blooms amid naked skeletal stems. It's a story where threats of violence are thwarted only by guns gone bad...or in the wrong room.

It begins innocently enough with a gardener's sneaking suspicions among this year's spring plantings: "Not cutworm nibblings. Their damage happens at ground level or below...Not starlings; they snip plants off an inch or so up... Rabbits can't reach this high..."

Here enters backstory in the form of last summer's devastation: a neat row of stems that were once young okra plants; pre-teen sunflowers, pulled down in their prime and rendered leafless; leafless squash plants resembling upside down umbrella prongs; even badly chewed tomato plants.

Characters in last summer's saga were a grown groundhog; her two offspring, Doofus and Bozo; the gardener and family. "Please say it's not...," moans the gardener this year, "...but it must be a groundhog!"

The next time she looks out a window, verification is openly grazing in the back yard. There's only one, but he's big. A new generation has come home all grown up. This calls for action.

By the time the BB gun is unearthed, this groundhog, which gets named Doofus, is rearranging the furniture in his ancestral home under the tool shed. There are other opportunities. But the BB gun, which eventually scared them off last year, is repeatedly out of pocket.

Doofus is, however, nervous. Every few bites, he sits up on his haunches — such a cute pose — to look around. It's a hoot to watch him, when chased out of the garden, flatten his fat self and squeeze under the tool shed door.

A week goes by and the veggie plants are dwindling. A sympathetic friend loans the gardener a pellet gun. Target practice goes well, first with the 'ping' of pellet hitting tool shed, then with the shudder of the more challenging geranium-leaf target. The gardener phones her aunt, who answers the 'how to cook a groundhog' question with: "I stewed them in water with salt and pepper."

The next time Doofus dines out, the pellet gun's arsenal has nothing left but a harmless 'click.' A trap is borrowed. It has metal bars that a critter can push to enter. Then the bars fall down and block the way out.

First baiting, Doofus reaches through the cage side to get the apple bits. "Let's see him pull half an apple out," growls the gardener. Soon, a brown furriness is inside the trap!

The gardener sees it, dons shoes, then looks out the window again. Doofus is outside the trap, chewing. Then back in, then out through the bars with the apple half. He sits on his haunches beside the cage, leisurely enjoying a healthy snack.

"I'm tired of being outsmarted by a furry rodent!" the gardener tells anyone who will listen at the store that sells traps. The top-of-the-line brand is expensive. But the clerk who demonstrated how to bait the cheaper model got his hand caught. And its instructions warn: "wear thick gloves to prevent being bitten by the caged animal."

The first time the trap is baited, Bingo!

It's a groundhog, all right. But it's barely half the size of Doofus… make that Mrs. Doofus. This explains why, earlier, she sat in the toolshed doorway, eying the trap with a worried look on her face. The gardener presumed she was trying to decide yet another angle to beat the humans at their own games.

The denouement: adorable Baby Bingo by now is hopefully reestablished in his own private tunnel alongside the country road where he was let loose.

As for Doofus? She packed up and left. Hopefully, forever.

End of story. Hopefully there will be no sequel.

Entrapment - Groundhog Finale

A large shadow was in the trap. Except shadows aren't furry.

It was mid August, I think, when my nephew Paul Donaldson left Columbia after a brief stay at our house. While here, he had repaired my ailing swing, which was good deed enough. But he also refurbished and set my thus far empty Have-a-Hart trap.

Using small tree limbs, he even built miniature rail fences leading to the trap's entrance. "Online information says guiding the creatures helps," he explained. Just before leaving for St. Louis, Paul added an irresistible serving of cantaloupe for bait. Then he placed tempting dibbles of the melon along the path between the wee fences.

All for naught. A day or so of near-100-degree weather must've made the cantaloupe resistible. No big deal. The garden was drying up to the point that no self-respecting groundhog would eat it anyway.

Fast forward to the afternoon of Saturday, September 3. Temperatures had at long last calmed to the point that I could enjoy an afternoon cup of coffee in the swing without melting. There was even a hint of a breeze.

In this 'all's right with the world' aura, I ambled over to the garden and stood idly beside scattered sticks that had been Paul's fences. "I ought to clean this up and put the trap away," I thought. Then I looked closer.

A large shadow was in the trap. Except shadows aren't furry. We had caught ourselves a genuine full-grown groundhog. One that liked dehydrated cantaloupe. I stared at it and it stared at me. Now what?

The logical next step was to cart G. H. off to a gardenless location and set him free. The carting, however, would be problematic. I'd seen a half grown groundhog intimidate a good-sized dog with its fierceness. Cage or not, I didn't want the varmint just a back seat away from the driver if that driver was me.

A couple of years ago, when the Have-a-Hart snagged a babe-in-arms groundhog, my neighbor who has a truck saved the day. I called him; he was down in his back. "Call Tennessee Wildlife," Jesse suggested. I looked them up and found only a Lewisburg listing. This being Saturday, they wouldn't be there anyway.

Halfway through placing a call to a relative with a truck, I remembered that he was recovering from an illness. Next followed a string of calls ending with "Leave your message after the beep." Somehow I didn't have a good feeling about getting a call-back to "Please come haul off this groundhog."

I was fast running out of truck-blessed friends. "I will do it myself," said the Little Red Hen. No, that was my voice. I picked up the trap, intending to set it near my non-truck vehicle so that, once a tarp was arranged, we'd be good to go.

My garden had served this critter well. It was heavy. Plus, its frantic running back and forth in the cage kept us both off-balance. A few feet into the effort, I gave up and went to enlist help. Jesse was on the phone, explaining my dilemma. "Here, talk to her," he said, and handed me the receiver.

Like our groundhog, the unlucky person on the line took the bait. Within the next hour or so, Jimmy and Kate Couch pulled into our driveway. We had a grand visit. When they left with a passenger in the truck bed, I waved gleefully.

The next time I talked to Jimmy, he said they let G. H. out in a rural area near a creek so it had water to drink. Our groundhog was in a better place.

Hopefully, G. H. was our last ever groundhog. Visually, a groundhog/woodchuck/gopher is cute, borderline cuddly. In a garden, however, it's a living, breathing threshing machine.

If nibbled pea vines ever hint that another is on board, I'll try to keep it out of both my garden and my column. There's a limit to how many marmot paw-prints readers will tolerate.

War

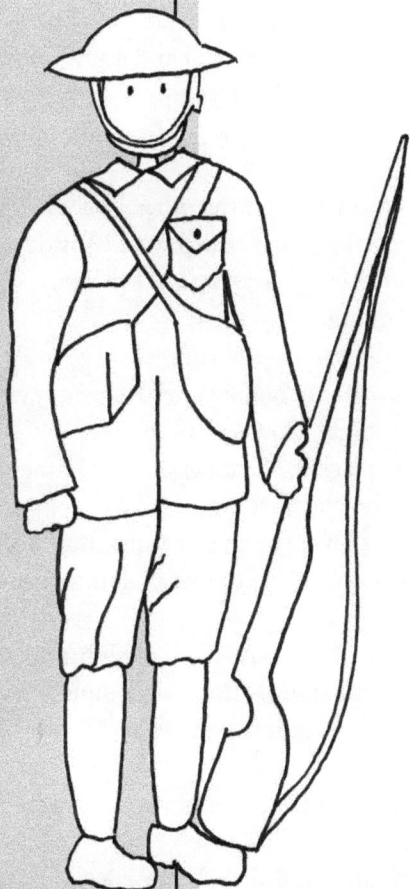

A Local Veteran's Memories of the Rohna Disaster

"After dark, they turned on landing lights and were strafing at us — killing a lot in the water."

Cleo Long's gentle voice and kind smile can't totally mask his apprehension about our pending interview. The 78-year-old veteran is about to share a secret he kept for 57 years.

He takes a deep breath and begins: "On November 26, 1943, my watch stopped at 13 minutes to 6:00. I'm assuming that's when I hit the water."

Cleo was a 19-year-old soldier aboard the Rohna, a British transport going from North Africa to Bombay, India. 'The water' was the Mediterranean Sea. "We'd just finished an air raid drill and gone below deck when the whistle went off again. I thought, 'Dry run.' I looked out through a porthole. A sergeant hollered, 'Get your d___ head out of that porthole! There's...'

"A bomb hit one side of the ship and went out the other. You coulda driven a transport truck through the holes. Steel beams were bent double all over. People were lying there dead. The stairway was blown away. People were screaming, hollering, begging."

Cleo pauses, says quietly, "I can still hear the screaming."

Survivors were told to jump overboard and get away as fast as they could; a lot of ammunition on board might blow up in the fires. A lieutenant offered Cleo $25 for his life jacket. "Lotta good that money woulda done me without the jacket," he chuckles.

Once Cleo was overboard, he went down a couple of times, but didn't reach bottom. "You talk about praying...you'll pray. I was talking to my mother and my dad..."

With about 25 others, he hung on to a lifeboat; 15-foot-high waves carried them out to sea instead of toward shore. "There were quite a few G planes. After dark, they turned on landing lights and were strafing at us — killing a lot in the water."

The Army estimated they were in the water 15 minutes. Cleo's estimate is 13 hours.

"There were only two of us left when a little British ship picked us up."

The other survivor was from Cleveland, Tennessee. "I tied the rope they threw us around the older man first." Cleo never saw the Cleveland man again.

"As they pulled me up the ship's side, a wave brought the lifeboat up and crushed me between it and the ship. When I came to, I was in a hospital. I kept asking for the Ray boy (his good friend from Ethridge). We were inducted together, went on furlough together..."

Cleo was reported MIA to his parents. At the African coast hospital where he was treated for a crushed back, the Red Cross said they didn't have permission to let his family know he was alive. "My parents didn't know different until January or February," he recalls.

The reason for the secrecy? "The Germans hit the Rohna with their new secret weapon, a radio-controlled bomb. Our army didn't want them to know how effective that weapon was."

Of 2,200 troops plus crew on the Rohna that day, 1,149 died; 1,103 of those were Americans. All 900-plus survivors had a secret to keep. "I went to a shrink before I left," Cleo says. "They tried to see if I knew anything of value."

When a medic told Cleo he was going home, he asked, "How?"

"Boat."

"No, sir," he said. "I either go by air or I'll stay here."

During the trip home, the airplane was grounded in Casablanca because President Roosevelt had just died. The next day, they flew in to Miami. "I kissed the ground," Cleo says.

After recuperation at Coral Gables and several transfers, Cleo was stationed in Bryan Field, Texas, until his discharge in late 1945. He got the Purple Heart and several medals, but no information about the Rohna. "I'd given up knowing anything about it," he says.

Cleo's grandson, Ronnie Long Jr. of Mt. Pleasant, didn't give up. He searched the internet. Not until 1996 did details about "U.S. Army's largest loss on the water of World War II" begin surfacing.

"The first information came from a Kentucky fellow who was originally on the Rohna, but was moved to a sister ship due to overcrowding," Cleo says. "He went back to Germany and talked to the pilot who dropped the bomb. After that, things just fell into place."

In October 2000, Congress passed Resolution #408 about the Rohna. A Rohna memorial has been built in Clanton, Alabama. Three books have been written on the disaster. Cleo thinks such publicity has 'brought it out' for survivors as well as for the general public. He adds, "To be frank, there's probably a lot that still hasn't come out."

His wife, Louise, notes that Cleo has never talked much about the Rohna. "I never wanted to talk about it afterwards," he says. "I just enjoyed being home. I wouldn't even think about it now if it weren't for my grandson…"

Since 1993, a Rohna Survivors Memorial Association has held reunions. Cleo would like to attend the one next week (May 3-6, 2001) in Arizona, but doesn't feel physically able.

Missing reunions is not Cleo's worst regret. He says, "I wish I'd gone to that Ray family down in Ethridge to tell them what happened to their son."

From 'Day of Infamy' to 'Day of Joy, Day of Fear'

The Spur station got broken into every week, not for the money, but to steal the ration stamps.

Herein are WWII impressions that lasted a lifetime, though at the time the two contributors were children. First, memories from Columbian Jesse Foreman, who grew up in the West Tennessee town of Humboldt:

On Sunday, Dec. 7, 1941, we were playing out in the yard when we realized something was going on. We ran to the porch, where the grown-ups were listening to the radio. There, we heard about Pearl Harbor being bombed.

On Monday, Dec. 8, they herded all of us — the entire elementary school — into the auditorium, where a radio was set up on stage. We listened to President Roosevelt's speech where he said, "…yesterday…a date which will live in infamy…" We also heard Congress declare war on Japan. As soon as the bell rang, every kid in the 3rd grade headed out the door to go enlist.

Our family lived next door to the bus station. The recruits heading out for camp filled up our front yard. We'd try to find a place to play and couldn't.

Families who had somebody in service were given a blue star to hang in their window. Blue stars were everywhere. If a soldier got killed, the family had a gold star. These kept popping up all over the neighborhood.

Everybody felt a part of the war effort…like it was up to all of us to do our part. We had a Victory Garden, which was like our before-the-war garden except it had a new name. For scrap iron drives, school kids would form teams. We'd haul the scrap iron in pushcarts and wagons to a collection site at school. Trucks would pick it up and carry it to make munitions.

Air raid wardens patrolled the neighborhood to be sure all the houses were blacked out. If we saw light leaking through windows, we would rap on the door and say, "You've got a leak. Cover it up."

Everything was rationed — sugar, cigarettes, butter, gasoline, coffee.

We got one pair of shoes a year for each family member. The Spur station got broken into every week, not for the money, but to steal the ration stamps. The thieves could sell them for good money.

Milan Arsenal was a big deal, bringing in thousands of workers from all over the country. There wasn't enough housing in that area, so the government hauled in pre-fab houses on trailer trucks. They'd put them up several per day. After the war was over, the government sold the houses to private owners.

As the war wore on, the U.S. began taking prisoners of war. Several hundred German POWs worked on farms near our town. We kids would watch them and try to talk to them. The older ones (in their 30's and 40's) who had lived before Hitler were nice.

The younger Hitler youth just sneered — a master race that wouldn't stoop to talking to American kids. I see why the Nazis were feared throughout the world.

I'd been reading about the atom as building blocks and felt like it had a lot of potential. I was working at a fertilizer plant part-time. An older boy came running in there, yelling, "They've dropped an atom bomb on Hiroshima!"

"A whattt?" somebody said…

This next account, "Day of Joy, Day of Fear," is from Effie Heiss, a native and longtime resident of Spring Hill who now lives in east Tennessee:

"The Japs have surrendered!" Everybody yelled it across the fence to each other. "Have ya heard? It's over! The War is over!!!"

Neighbor told neighbor; the mailman called it from each mailbox; someone drove down the road, blowing the horn and yelling, "The war is over. Our boys are coming home!"

My little brother slipped a cowbell over the handlebar of his tricycle and rode in big circles around the front yard, waving an American flag and shouting, "Yay, yay!"

I sat on the steps and waved my little flag. My parents and an aunt and uncle were just inside the door at the kitchen table. I could hear them talking.

"I heard that the smoke and fire went up as high as five miles and burned everything in sight for more than a hundred miles," Aunt Rachel said. "The atomic bomb, made right over there in Oak Ridge. William helped build some of them buildings."

"It killed a million people in just one minute," said Uncle Will.

"How can anybody make a bomb BIG enough to do that much damage?" Mama asked.

"It's not the size. It's something called a chain reaction," Daddy said. "One atom burns and causes the one next to it to burn and it just keeps burning for miles and miles."

"Well, wonder what's to keep the whole world from burning up," Mama said. "Everything is just atoms of some kind."

There in the hot August sun of 1945, a chill came over me. In the midst of rejoicing, I had a nagging fear. I sat on the step with my little flag, looking in the direction where I thought Japan would be, afraid that I would see the flames that would end the world...the same flames that had ended World War II.

From Badly Spelled Broccoli to Rice in Vietnam

"I'm going to ask you the same questions I've been asking the students all week,"
I warned him. "The difference is, your answers will be
within the context of Vietnam."

For two weeks, I've been writing with students at Elkton Elementary (K-8) in Giles County. To scratch the surface of getting to know them, I asked a few questions. Some results are: Predictably, pizza won out as a favorite food. As to the least-liked? By the second day I told them, "Don't worry about spelling. Broccoli has already been misspelled in every conceivable way."

Because last Thursday was Veteran's Day, I wanted to interview a veteran, and needed to find one onsite. Inquiries directed me to the school's guidance counselor, Doug Bassham.

"I'm going to ask you the same questions I've been asking the students all week," I warned him. "The difference is, your answers will be within the context of Vietnam."

What was your favorite food? Hmm. Over there? The things I couldn't have — hamburger, vegetables, fresh milk. Occasionally we'd get a hot meal. When that happened, my favorite thing was hot buttered rolls.

What was your least favorite food? RICE. The Vietnamese put a sauce on it, nook mam, that was liquid from decayed fish. That soured me on rice. I still won't eat it.

What was your favorite place? In Vietnam? On the airplane coming home. Seeing those harbor lights disappear…Now that I think about it, Cam Ranh Bay was a beautiful place.

What sound did you like to hear? Hmmm. The laughter of little kids in some of those villages. That was a really rare commodity. They were so sad.

What's a sound you didn't like to hear? Boys crying for their mama. The sounds of mortar and machine gun fire at 2:00 a.m.; the ungodly shrill sound of the siren going off if we got hit. The very boys who had cried for their mama or Jesus saying after all that, "Whoa! What a rush!"

What's something you were good at? Hmmm. Nothing really.

Hmmm…not being stupid. Not picking stuff up that might be booby-trapped. Watching where to put my feet. Hanging around guys who'd been there long enough that they knew the ropes. Not trying to be a Rambo or John Wayne hero. (pause) Writing home to keep my mom from worrying. Hmmm…(barely audible)…staying sane.

Beyond the questions, Doug described a few unforgettable scenes and circumstances:

The most disappointing thing I ever saw — They sent us down to a dock to pull security where some huge cranes were off-loading supplies. They kept unloading these box-like trailers like the ones trucks pull on highways. They all had 'Lady Bird Lines' written on their sides.

I asked my buddy "What's that about?"

"That's for her business over here," he said.

I wish I hadn't seen that. It made me angry.

I can see this scene as plain today as I saw it then. When I was leaving, my army buddies and I said our goodbyes, and they headed back to camp. I stood there waving at them as dust curled up around the back of their truck.

That army buddy bond, as any veteran knows, is unexplainable. It never goes away. There's a man in Georgia whose two sons are named Douglas and Eric – my names. My son is named after him.

As we waited to board the plane that would take us overseas, we had on shiny new green baseball caps, new jungle boots, new camouflage jungle fatigues. The guys who were getting off that plane had worn-out boots, fatigues that were faded almost white, battered hats. They were laughing at us because we had to go. How could they laugh at us?

A year later in Fort Lewis, Washington, we were getting off our plane dressed in our bedraggled outfits. I had just turned 20. The kids who were about to load up flocked around us like we were their grandparents or gurus, asking, "What's it like? What do we need to know?"

I could not laugh at them.

We gained almost 24 hours coming home. One day, I came out of the field in Vietnam nasty and dirty. A couple of days later, I was sitting in the living room at home with my parents, eating pinto beans and corn-bread, watching the war on TV. That was surreal.

Hmmm. The exhilarating feeling when the airplane that brought us back landed (on U.S. soil) was almost worth the whole thing. Almost. But not.

Disturbing Perspective on 9-11

*I have asked myself: If my spiritual leader had asked me
to do what the hijackers did, would I have followed through?*

*Shortly after the September 11, 2001 terrorist attacks, a friend penned a
letter that has haunted me ever since. Her perspective—that of a life-long
citizen of this "free" country who, nevertheless, grew up in a controlled and
controlling environment—was and is jolting. Here is her perspective:*

On September 11th two years ago I wept along with most of America
as I watched the smoke of the World Trade Centers fill my television
screen. But when people shook their heads in disbelief and wondered
how the suicide hijackers could think they were acting in the name of
God, I didn't. And when overnight our country became dotted with
American flags and almost every group who gathered sang God Bless
America, I was hesitant to join in.

The Taliban sends out only the news it wants its people to hear.
Like members of that society, I grew up with little exposure to outside
points of view. Our family read a church-owned newspaper, listened to a
church-owned radio station, and watched a church-owned television station. Despite growing up in America during the Viet Nam War, the Civil
Rights Movement and the Sexual Revolution, I was unaware that young
women my age were attending antiwar rallies and burning their bras.
This time in my life was spent in early morning religion classes, attending church retreats, and learning to sew modest clothes that would keep
young men from being tempted by my body.

Like those in the Al Qaeda network, I grew up with a strong devotion
to a spiritual leader. As a small child in Sunday School I sang songs that
committed me to follow him. As a teenager, I stood with other youth
in church and weekly repeated a pledge of loyalty to the church and our
leader.

Like the men who were willing to go to their grave to show their ex-
treme loyalty to bin Laden and his holy cause, I was reared to believe our
spiritual leader would never lead his flock astray. "And if he ever does,"
one friend reminded me, "the sin will be upon his head, not on ours. Our
duty is to follow."

Instead of terrorist tactics I was trained in the best ways to proselytize. As a teenager I feared for those in my school who were not part of God's true church. I imagined an eternity of Hell for them. To prevent this from happening, I invited many to visit our church. Four of my friends eventually joined. I felt relief for them and pride that I had 'saved' them.

Like the Al Qaeda network, the church in which I grew up has always gone to great lengths to keep its followers loyal. It strictly enforces a dress code, daily stresses the importance of obedience, directs high-ranking officials to follow the actions of suspected dissidents, and even censors its own history.

People rarely leave this church. However, following the death of my eldest daughter, its pat answers left me feeling empty and disillusioned. Despite knowing that I would bring shame to my family and friends, I began reading outside opinions and talking to non-members about their beliefs. After several years my questions finally led me to do the unpardonable; I said, "I don't believe" (the church's doctrines).

At best my friends and family now consider me deluded; at worst, a follower of Satan.

Several times since September 11th (2001), I have asked myself: If my spiritual leader had asked me to do what the hijackers did, would I have followed through? If I truly felt I was specially selected, and if I truly thought the people he told me to kill were evil, could I have done something this heinous?

The truth is, I'm not sure what I would have done. And that terrifies me.

Because of living so many years in a subculture where many freedoms we enjoy as Americans were denied me, I have other fears as well. I worry that in our country's eagerness to be united and stand behind our President, we will become afraid to voice dissenting opinions. I am leery of single-mindedness wherever it is found. Even too much patriotism can be dangerous.

I hope that, if this conflict continues, we will make a conscious effort as a nation to consider many points of view. We are now living with the daily fear of what someone else may do to us, but perhaps the greatest enemy we face could be what we do to ourselves.

Recent
History

Tuesday, September 11, 2001

Everything is different. Out of kilter.

On the one hand, coverage of this week's events has been so comprehensive, further input is redundant. On the other hand, there is no other subject this week. Is there a U.S. citizen anywhere who is not still reeling from the news?

Three friends from various parts of New York, the state, have been in touch to say they're okay. The one who lives near Syracuse says: "On this morning's news they ran a list of the known passengers on the flights that crashed. One was a four-year-old girl. Who can begin to understand the atrocity of a human being who could watch that little girl board that plane, knowing he planned to explode it into a skyscraper one hour later?"

Mary, a friend who lives 20 blocks north of the World Trade Center area reports: "My neighbor climbed up the fire escape to watch. All around, people were standing on rooftops with their heads in their hands, staring in disbelief."

Her husband rushed by bicycle to get one child at the United Nations school, afraid that building might be targeted next, while she ran to another school to collect their kindergartener. On her way, "I saw masses of people all walking north covered in dust."

Mary alternated between watching the real thing and watching TV coverage. She describes the scene below 14th Street: "…all you see are army trucks and fighter jets, police blockades, mortuary trucks." When Wednesday's news stated that the constantly swirling dust/smoke cloud was full of asbestos, her family left the city.

A somewhere-in the-Catskills New York friend visited the city last weekend. She reminisces: "Sunday evening, my husband Mark and I were standing on the newly opened pedestrian path on the Manhattan bridge, admiring the sunset light on the NYC skyline…"

They know three people who got out of the World Trade Center. One was on the 89th floor; the plane hit at about the 91st. "She walked barefoot all the way to her dad's place uptown. Somebody offered her a pair of sneakers."

Our TV screens are now full of images of bone-tired rescue workers. Sometimes they create human assembly lines to move mountains of rubble, one steel slab/crushed computer at a time. Concurrently, folk hundreds of miles removed from the actual scene are emotionally trying to pick up the pieces, to reassemble.

Everything is different. Out of kilter. The cat shouldn't still judge the state of the world by what's in her supper dish. During my 30-mile trip to Pulaski Tuesday evening to play hymns for a prayer service, the sky was a sparkling blue dotted with puffy white clouds. Its beauty and serenity seemed a mockery of reality, almost sacrilegious. Wednesday night's lashing, snarling, roaring thunderstorm better represented its moment in time. As did Thursday's sky — no color; no identifiable clouds; just a grayish white void stretching as far as the eye could see.

At a Thursday evening rehearsal of the Columbia Chorale, director Marsha Scheusner voiced similar sentiments: "I was dragging myself to a children's choir practice, thinking how trivial the rehearsal and everything else we're doing is, in light of what's happened."

Then, to the assembled singers, she said, "I was wrong. What we're doing right now is vitally important. It's exactly what we should be doing — working together at what we love; learning to depend on and trust each other's ability to do their part; enjoying each other's company. This is what it's all about."

What it's all about — normalcy — has, in varying degrees, been shattered for us all. My email friends are asking, "Will we ever be safe again?" "What now?" We all are asking. These great unanswerables roll toward us like the all-enveloping debris clouds we see in replays of the imploding towers.

Yet, as long as a bystander offers a pair of sneakers to a barefoot passerby as she stumbles away from danger, there is hope.

A First Flight Soon After the September 11, 2001 Attacks

Everyone, even the crew, was totally tense.
It was very quiet. No one joked. No one smiled.
The flight attendants had tears in their eyes.

Beckie Weinheimer lives in a community near Washington D.C. In late August, her daughter, Holly Kearl, had left for her first semester at a California college. Holly was to be on the school's cross-country track team, so arrived early for training.

Beckie had a Sept. 14 plane ticket to California, with a stopover in Texas, to help Holly settle in. Especially after the attacks, Beckie wanted to make that trip.

She recalls, "I stood at the Dulles airport most of the day Friday (Sept. 14). There was no way I was going to get on a flight. Mine, along with everything else, was canceled. Holly didn't want me to risk the trip. My husband Alan Kearl, after spending hours trying to get me a ticket, asked me to give up. But I was on some automatic adrenaline. I couldn't give up. I didn't know why, but come hell or high water, I was going to California.

"This one airline worker. I don't know why he picked me to help; he must have seen the look of determination in my eyes, and connected with it on some level. He broke all the rules — left his post at ticketing and walked me and my bags through to a special security; asked them to try to get me on a flight. They plugged away at their computers and said no, no. He said, 'Try again. Try this and see if it will allow her in.'

"The plane was scheduled to leave in a few minutes. He kept at it and they got me through. I believe we were the first flight to Los Angeles out of Dulles (the intended route of the plane that hit the Pentagon) after the attacks.

"I was scared to death to fly from Dulles to LA. And more so when I actually got on the plane and felt the mood. Everyone, even the crew, was totally tense. It was very quiet. No one joked. No one smiled. The flight attendants had tears in their eyes. We figuratively held our breath for the five-plus hours it took.

"My commuter flight to San Francisco was much easier. Everyone was vocal about being scared. They joked. They clapped when we landed. The flight attendant, in her usual in-flight safety talk, acknowledged our fears."

Beckie rented a car in San Francisco and drove to her destination. She says, "My luggage, of course, didn't make it until the night before I left to come back."

Because of practice schedules and freshman orientation, Beckie's time with Holly was limited during the short visit. Beckie 'didn't have a clue' why, for such a brief stay, she had risked the flight.

The courier who delivered her luggage drove up from LA. "He wanted to hear my story — had been asking everyone. He handed me my suitcase and asked why I had come out. With my luggage in hand, I finally knew why.

"I patted the suitcase and said, 'Inside here I have a flight coupon for my daughter who just started college a continent away from us. I have a similar coupon at home, so both of us can know we are only a flight away. Five hours. Any day. Any time. And we can be together.'

"Then I broke down. 'Damn it, someone tried to rob me of that security. All of a sudden, my daughter might as well be in the Sudan. And I wasn't about to have that security taken away from me or from her. I wanted Holly to know I was still only five hours away.' I smiled at the courier. 'It took a few more than five hours this time, but I think she's got the idea.'"

Beckie was hoping for an easier flight back to D.C., but it wasn't to be. "The flight was full. I sat with an 83-year-old woman and a man who was definitely middle-eastern. All the time I was in California and saw Muslims, I smiled; was extra polite if they waited on me in stores. But when I was sitting on the plane, I wished he wasn't there. I thought about how I would protect myself and the elderly lady next to me. And I hated that I did that — had a plan in my head. That I didn't trust him just because of his nationality."

Now that Beckie is safely home, she writes, "We have planes flying overhead that never used to fly. I can hear them loud and clear inside with the doors and windows all shut. My friend reminds me that I'm probably safer with them flying, but I would rather rewind to before September 11 when I walked around in ignorant, unprotected bliss."

Wouldn't we all?

'Miracle on the Hudson' Revisited

In seconds, water rose from Vallie's ankles to her neck.

On January 15, 2012, for the second time Vallie Collins sat down in her assigned seat in the backmost row of U. S. Airways flight #1549. This time, a museum curator advised Vallie and her seatmate to "Please keep your feet on the footrest. What's left of the floor back here is paper thin."

Not comforting news, but preferable to what they'd heard in those same seats exactly three years earlier, which was: "This is the captain. Brace for impact." On that day, shortly after takeoff from LaGuardia Airport, Vallie, who was in an aisle seat, heard a loud 'thunk.'

"What was that?" she asked her seatmate, who was looking out the window.

"Geese," he said. Soon, flames were coming out of the engine.

Vallie was a frequent flyer. Once during a turbulent flight, she was very nervous. Her seatmate that day was a pilot. "We're okay," he assured her. "All we pilots worry about is birds and fire."

On January 15, 2009, flight #1549 had both. Vallie and 149 other passengers followed instructions from the crew of how to brace for their crash landing in the Hudson River.

After the impact came chaos. "People were screaming, clogging the aisles, even getting luggage," Vallie remembered. She was at the back of the plane trying, against intense water pressure, to help the crew open the rear exit.

In seconds, water rose from Vallie's ankles to her neck. "I took up the flight attendants' chant: 'Go to the wings' and struggled uphill in that direction. My calling out the instructions wasn't heroic. Those people were in my way!"

Like the other passengers, Vallie climbed out onto a wing. From there, she was able to get onto a life raft. Stretching across the water, a mother handed her little girl Sophia from the wing to Vallie.

"Sophia's quietness forced me to get calm," Vallie said. "And her sharp teeth as she chewed on my arm through my sweater kept me in touch with reality."

The best part of that reality was seeing a ferry named Thomas Jefferson about 400 yards away, chugging toward the plane. It was leading a pack of first responders. "Those first responders," said Vallie, "saved us. The plane sank within 24 minutes of landing on the water; we were all rescued in 17 minutes."

Of course, the landing know-how of the flight's captain, Chesley Burnett "Sully" Sullenberger, made the rescue possible. He later told interviewers, "Every flight I ever flew, since age 16, prepared me for that moment."

Vallie, like many of the rescued, was soaked and trembling from head to toe. During the two hours of processing at the ferry terminal, she received size 48 pants for her slender frame, but the pants were dry.

"Somebody had foresight to go buy a big package of tube socks," she said. "If I'd had it, I would have paid a million dollars for that pair of socks."

In the days following the crash, Vallie vowed not to let the fear win. So five days later, she was on a plane en route to appearing on the Ellen DeGeneres show. Her determination was bolstered by advice from her grandmother, Kathryn O'Guinn: "If you run away from one thing, you're gonna run into something else."

Perhaps that same logic is why, on the third anniversary of the crash landing on the Hudson, Vallie and 51 other passengers accepted an invitation to revisit #1549. After the accident, the Carolinas Aviation Museum in Charlotte, North Carolina had arranged to acquire the plane's entire airframe as a donation from the aircraft's insurer, and worked toward reconstructing it in the Carolina Air Museum.

Reconstruction was not quite complete in time for the anniversary revisit, so only one wing was attached. Vallie's seven-year-old son, noticing this, said, "Mama, no wonder that plane crashed. It only had one wing!"

Vallie's life has been profoundly affected by surviving 'The Miracle on the Hudson.' During a recent talk at Highland Park Baptist Church in her hometown of Columbia, TN, where her parents Kaye and Phain Smith and her sister Shea Truitt still live, she shared how the experience has changed her sense of life purpose:

Vallie seeks, as much as possible, to live at peace. "I have a whole new scale of how to get upset," she said. "'Don't sweat the small stuff' really kicks in."

After undergoing treatment for post-traumatic stress disorder (PTSD), Vallie promotes empathy with the reminder that, "Somebody may look just fine on the outside..."

Another insight is her perspective on the importance of physical fitness. "You don't know when you'll find yourself in a life-threatening situation."

Vallie praised U. S. Airways for their follow-up after the accident. Passengers were reimbursed for lost luggage and ticket monies. "We even got 14 frequent flyer miles," she said with a smile.

Several months after the crash, passengers' belongings, except for medicines, cosmetics, and such that would be bio-hazards, were returned. "I got individually sealed expired coupons," Vallie noted.

In a phone conversation with a worker at the restoration business that was processing the belongings, Vallie said, "Cleaning up and packaging all our stuff must be tiresome, tedious work."

"This one is the best project ever," replied the worker. "It's the first time we're not sending the items to victims' families."

Music

Challenges of Church Choir Membership

For once, there was a valid reason for the choir's tardiness.

At gatherings such as the Montreat Conference on Music and Worship, when it's time to sing, a choir of consenting adults rises as one body. After the anthem ends, everyone sits down. This is as it should be. It is also not the norm as I have come to accept it.

I have been involved with church choirs ever since I could see over the choir loft rail. Their repertoires and abilities ranged from impressive to so-so. The one universal trait they shared? Their inability to conquer physical challenges such as sitting, standing, getting into the choir loft, and — heaven help us — processing down the aisle.

Any choir that processes is an 'accident looking for a place to happen.' Complications abound — bifocals, flowing robes, steps to negotiate, directions to turn, notes to sing, plus seasonal hazards like palm branches and candles.

A choir that simply appears in the loft near the appropriate time should have no logistical traumas, right? Strike the adverb 'simply.'

In my current situation, when the organist (me) chimes the hour — 10:30, ten chimes — for the worship service to begin, the first chime should cause doors on opposite sides of the choir loft to creak open. There should be footsteps as half of a choir row emerges from each door, walks in, and meets in the middle.

Though this is a sound theory, it seldom happens. Last Sunday, for the second time in three weeks, instead of footsteps, I heard whispers and frantic scurrying. Judging by the number of hours I chimed, the choir finally took its place at 15:30 o'clock. For once, there was a valid reason for the choir's tardiness: when the first person tried to open the door to the choir loft, the doorknob fell into her hand.

At one church where I was organist, the organ console made it possible for me to witness each step of whatever choir-entry drama was unfolding. Everything hinged on getting the first two women through the doors (men never led; their challenge was to follow). The steps leading to the choir loft were narrow and winding.

Often, just as the first robed female in high heels and a tight skirt wended her way to the top step juggling a hymnal, bulletin, and folder full of music, someone decided another person should lead in. The ex-leader had to climb down as her replacement ascended, creating a potential for disaster that would thrill a movie producer.

Assuming the leader of the moment did eventually get to the front of the pack, a new problem arose. She needed to make eye contact with the leader on the other side so that, by silent agreement, they entered the loft simultaneously. The leader across the way invariably was (a) in deep conversation with the person behind her, (b) totally immersed in reading the announcements, or (c) staring into space.

On a rare lucky day, she would awake to the real world, make the prerequisite eye contact, and step into the choir loft only slightly flustered. More likely, her counterpart had to send a stage-whispered S.O.S. to the last person in her line, who galloped around to send the whisper up the other row of stalled choir members. Someone near the front would poke the errant leader, causing her to leap into the choir loft while the leader across the way still waited for eye contact.

Since both leaders by then were nearly galloping, the congregation eagerly anticipated a collision. Sometimes they were not disappointed.

Thus begins many a church choir's participation in worship. In a changing world, this is one scenario I predict will be eternal. I further believe that, of all the aspects of worship, the Almighty Ear is tuned to the choirs of our culture. Not because of tonal purity, but to find out what in heaven's name will happen next.

At-the-Console Wedding Woes

The guy involved is lucky to have escaped the mother of the bride and me without a trumpet wrapped around his windpipe.

Any church organist who goes to hell will spend eternity playing weddings. Every bride will have at least three mothers take it upon themselves to supervise the selection of music. Every wedding will have a minimum of 14 attendants; half of those will be four years old or younger. The aisle they walk down will be the length of a football field. Blocking the organist's view of the procession will be a pulpit, several groomsmen, candelabra, flowers, and a choir rail. A well-meaning soloist will give confusing signals as to whether all those mothers are seated.

If for no other reason, church organists need to behave themselves.

Wedding woes for an organist can begin with selection of the music. My first choice is a bride who has given no thought to it; she can select from my repertoire. Next in my good graces is the bride who wants favorites from her background in church. My own repertoire has been enriched by searching out such hymns and, yes, youth anthems for inclusion in wedding programs. Sometimes fresh ideas for processionals and recessionals present themselves in this context.

Absolutely off the list of favorites is the couple that arrives armed with a list of top tens from the hard rock hall of fame. It's a tie as to which is worse, facing them with the church's refusal to allow such music; or, if it's a church that doesn't care, trying to tuck a few of their favorites in without barfing on the keyboard.

If a vocalist is part of a church wedding's music, lyrics should be appropriate if read from the pulpit. Sometimes, instrumentalists other than the organist are involved. Flutes are pretty adaptable; brass often aren't. When working with brass, I seem to bring on my own disasters by assuming. Anything. Like that they hear what I say. Or that I give a sensible answer to their questions.

In one brass-situation-from-hell, the guy involved is lucky to have escaped the mother of the bride and me without a trumpet wrapped around his windpipe. That mother, in an effort at perfection, bypassed local offerings and hired an out-of-town 'professional musician.' I called to arrange a time we could practice; he wasn't interested. Nor did he wish to arrive early enough to rehearse before the wedding itself.

The day of the wedding, I was well into the prelude music when he sauntered into the choir loft, rattled open the trumpet case, blew air through the instrument to warm it up, and considered himself ready for Purcell's Trumpet Voluntary.

He wasn't. Some notes cracked, others were missed. He flubbed entrances, and was badly out of tune with the organ. After the service, he sheepishly admitted, "This isn't the horn I usually play. It hasn't been out of the case in a month." As if we didn't know already.

Later, the bride's mother said, "I told him he should be embarrassed to accept my money because he ruined my daughter's wedding." He took the money.

Strange problems happen at weddings. Sometimes they necessitate lengthening the music played prior to the ceremony. One wedding delay was based on bouquets. Somehow, the florist had gotten the wrong count on bridesmaids. Not until they were lined up and receiving their flowers did anyone realize the mistake.

Frantic calls to the flower shop went unheeded; the workers were there, but it was past closing time, so they didn't answer the phone. The florist had to rush to his shop, build a bouquet, and rush back while, naturally, organ music filled in the time.

Not all 'strange problems' occur on the big day itself. Recently, a bride whose hecticity caused her to cancel a couple of music-selecting sessions called. "Could we possibly plan the music over the phone?" she asked. It's the first time I ever tried to sing Bach's Prelude and Fugue in C Major. Those trills are murder.

Despite horror stories, it's time to admit that, for every problem wedding I've played through the years, there've been a dozen pleasant ones. So if anyone who's hired me as organist for a wedding happens to read this, consider yourself among those dozens!

Missing a Beat While Marching to Zion

Not a breath of air was stirring, but I needed every possible advantage.
So I pinned the music to the stand anyway.

I don't know how it is at your church on Wednesday nights. At ours, beginning at 5:00 p.m., choir practices rotate with classes for children and youth. Next, all ages come together for an evening meal. Then we again disperse to choirs, classes, and Bible study.

The evening feels strongly of shared faith, family, and friendship. Most of the time, the schedule flows along reasonably well. But a few weeks ago, it didn't.

The music part of the equation began, as usual, with a choir peopled with 2nd through 4th graders. Since they were to sing in the following Sunday's service, this was an especially important rehearsal.

Only three of the regular singers showed up. Near the end of our time together, a mother arrived to explain that, in an after-school cross-country event, the very children who made up that choir had been scheduled last. Hence, the absences.

After dinner, a pre-school choir and handbell players began practicing. Those rehearsals must not have gone perfectly either because, as the adult choir assembled, someone's aside to me was, "Can anything else go wrong?"

Well, yes, it could. This night was special. Rather than having the usual rehearsal, our choir was to sing at a tent revival. Many among us had never even been to a tent revival, so mixed in with our appreciation of the invitation was some apprehension as to whether we'd do okay.

My apprehension led the pack. We were to sing a version of "Marching to Zion" that was accompanied, not by keyboard, but with drum. Thanks to everyone with expertise turning us down, I'd been assigned the role of drummer. Over fifty years had passed since my dismal career as a percussionist in the local high school band. Since then, there'd been a brief period of playing tympani in a community band. But snare drum? Today's drummers don't even hold the sticks the way I was taught.

Before heading to the revival, the choir and I mutually survived a final run-through of "Marching…" Then three gallant guys carried the drum,

drum stand, and music stand for me. All I had to keep up with were my purse, the drumsticks, and the music. Due to memories of long ago out-door concerts in windy conditions, I took clothespins to secure the music to the stand.

Our hosts greeted us kindly, the state-of-the-art tent had plenty of room for us, and there was ample time to set up before the service began. Not a breath of air was stirring, but I needed every possible advantage. So I pinned the music to the stand anyway.

At the appointed time in the service, the choir assembled and our director set the tempo. The anthem began with nothing but drum. I had those first few measures memorized, so I watched the director instead of looking at the music. A few measures into the song, I did glance at my music. The notes looked different than ever before.

"Something is wrong here," I realized. Still faking a drum part poorly, I looked farther down the page. At the very bottom, the title was looking up at me. I had pinned the music to the stand upside down.

By then, though the choir was singing a part where the drum should have been silent, I was still frantically drumming. I tried to fade away graciously, unpinned and righted the music, and searched it for my next entrance. From that point on, the drum part more or less resembled what was on the now right-side-up page.

But was permanent damage done to my chances of arriving at Zion? That remains to be seen.

An Auctioned Recital Reaps Unexpected Rewards

*For me, the real reward was the response
from people who lined up afterward.*

In January of 2000, I entered a two-year graduate writing program at Vermont College in Montpelier. It was one of those low residency deals — less than two weeks on campus twice a year. Between times, we sent writings by mail/email to our faculty advisor for critiques and guidance.

The campus' large gathering place had a pipe organ that was beautiful to look at, and passing fair sound-wise. Early on, I got permission to play the thing. So I fiddled with it during rare pockets of free time.

One feature of that first residency was the program's annual Scholarship Auction. This being a writing community, offerings other than what you'd expect at a generic auction were up for grabs. Faculty members' free manuscript critiques brought top dollar, as did signed copies of books whose authors were likely a row or so away.

The next residency, which was in July, I again found time to play the campus' pipe organ. This time, I'd brought music from my repertoire and busied myself figuring out suitable registrations (sound combinations that best complement what's on the page).

As the summer session wrapped up, we were reminded to bring donations in January for the auction. Since students and faculty hailed from all over, items that identified our 'home base' were encouraged.

"Aha!" thought I. "A Polk Home cookbook…"

I arrived on campus in January 2001 with the cookbook in tow. Also, I'd again packed organ music. As I revisited the sounds and songs I'd worked on the previous summer, an off-the-wall idea came to mind: would anyone at the auction bid on a program of organ music?

The thought wouldn't go away. So despite trying to talk myself out of it, I added that option to the auction's offerings. The evening of the auction, I left before my mini-recital came up for bidding. Turns out, the faculty pooled their resources, bought the recital, and on the spot figured out a time for it, pending my okay.

At the program, I introduced the selections in groupings. After the first 'set,' I turned to the audience to announce the next. A classmate sitting near the front was not just crying; she was weeping uncontrollably. As the program progressed, she stayed in meltdown. I'm not a great organist, but I knew my playing itself was not the cause.

Counting donations at the door, the program netted $150 for the scholarship fund. But for me, the real reward was the response from people who lined up afterward. A divorced faculty member whose former spouse was a minister said, "Thank you. I have not returned to church since our divorce, and it's the music that I miss most." A student who had to ride a motorized cart around campus because of a crippling disease that attacked her in adulthood said, "I enjoyed this so much. It reminded me of when I could play music like that."

My friend who wept apologized profusely. Her immediate family had recently defected from the religious sect she and her husband were raised in. She had shared with me some of the resulting angst and bitterness. "There's something good about everything," she said in explaining her tears. "What's good about our former church is its rich music tradition. And this brought that back."

So what does all this have to do with Christmas? Not much. Except that the January recital in Vermont was as near to 'marching with the little drummer boy' as I'll ever get. Remember him? He had no gift to give the Newborn King, so he played his drum, and that turned out to be even better than okay.

The moral of this story: Like the little drummer boy, if we try to talk ourselves out of sharing whatever gifts are ours to offer, we need to not listen, at Christmas or whenever.

Keeping Up Appearances

Woes of Those Who Can't Accessorize

*A young woman who was walking by glanced my way, did a double-take,
then walked purposefully toward me.*

On the fringes of our population cringes a small band of folk who try to remain invisible fashion-wise because they are accessorizingly challenged. The malady that makes one eligible for membership in this group is neither genetic nor catching; there is currently no known cure.

Symptoms vary. One is sloppy scarves. Those of us thus afflicted admire from afar anyone who can get through a day — heck, an hour — with a knotted or flowing scarf highlighting their outfit. For us, that option is out.

Case in point: Years ago, I worked down the hall from she who often wore scarves which looked as nice at the end of the day as when she'd first walked in the door. The scarves languishing in a drawer at home began to haunt me.

"Mind over matter," I decided. One brave day, I told the attractively scarfed one, "Tomorrow, if you will monitor and repair it every hour on the hour, I will wear a scarf."

I did; she didn't. The venture became a wadded, wrinkled failure.

Another symptom can pop up in the form of wandering necklaces. The wearers leave home with the fastener in back where it belongs. By the time they get where they're going, their pulse has propelled the clasp front and center.

"Aha!" comes the cry from well-wishers hoping to cure the affliction. "Perhaps longer, heavier necklaces will work!" Good plan. But we in the trenches have trouble even with those sturdy contenders. An example from my own case history comes to mind:

My daughter gave me a pendant composed of a rose-colored rock artfully entwined with a decorative silver band. It matched several outfits, and immediately became a great favorite.

One trip, I was waiting in line in a crowded airport, secretly secure in the fact that my ensemble included an appropriate accent. A young woman passing by glanced my way, did a double-take, then walked purposefully toward me. Gently lifting the rose stone of my necklace, she turned it over. "This is the way it should be," she said. As she disappeared into the milling crowd, she added, "I know about these things."

Bracelets behave better. But heavier ones have been known, at the most inopportune moments, to break their clasps and hurl themselves across rooms. The obvious solution — safety chains — delight in snagging garments, their high particular being knit sweaters.

The accessories mentioned thus far, if we're brutally honest, are dispensable. But shoes, in our culture, are pretty much a must. Without even factoring in comfort, shoes can cramp the accessory-challenged.

Mysterious rules govern shoe decisions. Dark won't do with light clothing; yet, time of year trumps the dark/light factor. No matter the clothing's shade, she who wears white shoes after Labor Day might as well disentangle herself from society as we know it.

Another debatably necessary accessory is the seemingly passive pocketbook. Purse size is important. One that's too small won't hold bare essentials, but the huge shoulder-strapped version can weigh enough to cause back pain. Any size purse has the uncanny ability to hide a half-pound ring of keys under a postage stamp.

A recent sticky addition to purse problems is Velcro. Hopefully, every manufacturer who uses this option for purse closure will, at some public performance, sit next to a lady who must noisily rip Velcro apart to reach each mint and tissue she needs.

When said lady excuses herself at intermission, we'll cheer if that Velcro fastening pops open and spills the purse's contents into that already frazzled manufacturer's lap.

Somewhere in the debris will be proof that the offending purse belongs to a card-carrying member of the Accessorizingly-Challenged.

A House-Hunter's Guide to Pointy-Eared Problems

The pesky varmints I refer to are seldom if ever seen.
So it's hard to recognize an infestation ahead of time.

I recently accompanied a family on a house-hunting expedition. We checked out the crawl space and ceiling height; roof age; proximity to heavy traffic and other undesirables.

We peered at plumbing and inspected basements for leaks. I learned what to look for, in the unlikely event I ever house-hunt.

I even learned of scams to avoid, such as this classic:

The homeowners, as requested, left at the time prospective buyers were to inspect their house...except for one elderly lady who was presumed too frail to bother with the exodus. The ancient one stayed in a living room rocking chair. Each time the house-hunters made their rounds, there she sat — rock, rock, rocking in her chair.

Perhaps the homey touch of that old lady in the rocker swayed them. Whatever the reason, the house sold to those buyers. During their move, the new owners discovered that, where the rocking chair had been, there was a large stain on the otherwise new-looking carpet.

I am grateful for the learning experience afforded by tagging along on my friends' house-hunts. But their logical endeavors take a back seat to what I wish *I* had looked for. Every single time I've moved, innocent-looking houses turn out to be crammed to the gills with pests. Not the usual mice, squirrels, and bugs. The pesky varmints I refer to are seldom if ever seen. So it's hard to recognize an infestation ahead of time.

It's only after closets are in use that one type — the scramblers — let themselves be known. Clues show up quickest in the linen closet. Non-linens creep in — hair dryers, household cleaners, fingernail polish. Then one day, recently folded and stacked towels are mysteriously disheveled.

A glance into the formerly organized coat closet discloses sleeping bags, stadium seats, and a cat where umbrellas are supposed to be. Further inspection discovers that the closet floor is a sea of single shoes pining for their mates. This evidence will stand up in court as testament that the house is infested with closet scramblers.

Another invisible household pest is the dish dirtier. Where these abound, a family can leave a perfectly clean kitchen and return to find dirty dishes littering the counter and table. Once they have a foothold, dish dirtiers can even thrive side by side with electric dishwashers.

Kin to the closet scramblers, but more versatile, are the clutterbugs. These little devils delight in strewing things throughout the house. A living room with tennis balls, lipsticks, and socks displayed as prominently as photos is a success story for clutterbugs. They also relish chairs piled high with magazines and unmentionables.

What the clutterbugs miss, the floor flubbers tend to. This breed is especially fond of leaving shoes in trip-overable places. Allegedly, they will fight a clutterbug to the death for the right to stray sandals.

Every house I've ever lived in was teeming with these critters. And though I've never seen them, I'd know one in an instant. Their ears are pointed. Their thick skin, like a chameleon's, can change colors to merge with the locale. They wear tiny quiet shoes that are never removed, for fear floor flubbers will steal them. (Even the floor flubbers keep their shoes on, considering the fierce competition between tribes.) Their eyes are wee slits that don't glow. They grin constantly, from the sheer fun of their work.

There's no spray or trap on the market to rid a house of these pests. Perhaps moving is a solution. But chances are, they'd sneak into the boxes.

I've coexisted with clutterbugs and their ilk for so long, I'm resigned to their mischief. But a word to realtors: if evidence of any of the above surfaces in a house you're about to show, hide it.

And to potential buyers: forget window types and heat/air systems. It's the invisible pointy-eared ones that'll make or break your long-term comfort.

Splitting Hairs Over
"Does She or Doesn't She"

"Is there such a color as dishwater brown?"
I asked my hair stylist.

I'm minding my own business, getting a drink at a water fountain. My brother is next in line. I like to think it was an ultra-strong ray of sunshine zooming in on my head that inspired him to burst into song. This song: "The old gray mare, she ain't what she used to be…"

I mentioned the graying to a friend whose hair turned when she was in her early 30's. She warned, "If you decide to color it, get it done soon. By the time I considered it, it was too late."

I ignored her advice. After all, in my mirror at home, encroaching grays seemed to be in the minority. Once when three of us were sharing that mirror I told the others, "My hair doesn't look gray to me in THIS mirror."

She on my left, whose real color was a distant memory, said, "Mine never looked gray in MY mirror, either."

She on my right, making sure she had eye contact with me in that loyal mirror, stated firmly, "Trust me. Your hair is gray. In this and all mirrors."

Thus began agonizing about whether or not to dye. "Is there such a color as dishwater brown?" I asked my hair stylist. "That's what mine seems to be stuck at."

"It's mousy," he replied in a voice choking with the pent-up emotion of finally saying what he thought. Instead of whapping him, I said, "Okay. Let's go with the fake stuff."

"Color enhancement," he corrected me.

A lot of adjectives could be applied to the result of that decision. Subtle was not among them. During those first couple of weeks when I was new to the ranks of the color enhanced, I got numerous double-takes from people who saw me all the time.

The ones I didn't see often were more fun. When my path crossed that of my father's neighbor, he said, "You look younger every time I see you." When a member of choirs past and I had a rare meeting, she asked,

"What's happened? You look younger."

I confessed. "Well, whatever it is, keep it up!" she advised.

During that period of adjustment, I began seeing the hair shades of others in a whole new light. Not just teens with purple, green, chartreuse dye jobs. I became suspicious of the golden, amber, or raven tresses of some young women — and men — whose hues I'd previously considered natural.

Though for now I'm taking the advice to 'keep it up,' a student's essay haunts me. In it, he berated his elders for trying to camouflage their graying locks. "Turning gray is a natural part of the aging process, and nobody ought to be ashamed of it," he wrote while perched beneath his full head of curly teen blondness.

The polar opposite opinion was voiced by a friend. When she first saw my new look, she vowed, "As long as hair color is in bottles on the store shelves, I'll never be gray!"

I'm not sure if that will be my stance. But this isn't the time to agonize about it. It might make me late for today's appointment with he who wields the color-enhancement wand.

Gifts Gone Awry

"When I saw what it was," she recalled, "I almost threw it at him."

'Twas the era when our oldest two children were preschoolers, with all the clutter and chaos inherent where that age is housed. Yet Jesse, perhaps due to frequent reminders, remembered my birthday.

Someone at the store where he bought the gift had wrapped it for him. The package looked really nice, but its size and shape didn't correspond with any of the hints I'd dropped.

The reason? It was a waffle iron.

At that point in life, getting the simplest of meals on the table was a coup. I not only didn't know how to make waffles; I wasn't eager to learn.

My face must have mirrored that sentiment.

"While the clerk was wrapping it," Jesse said, "she asked me if you wanted a waffle iron." His response had been, "No, but she ought to."

At our next yard sale, somebody got a real bargain on a shiny new you-guessed-it.

A friend experienced a similar letdown when, for a special occasion, her husband gave her what he must have thought was a delightful set of pans. She managed to accept them with more grace than my reaction to the waffle iron, and mentally masked her disappointment with "there's always next time…"

When next time arrived, the husband had decorated her gift in wild excess. But its shape provided no hint as to contents. After numerous wrong guesses, the baffled wife gave up and opened the package. "When I saw what it was," she recalled, "I almost threw it at him."

He'd given her an electric mini-vac.

These experiences bring to mind an observation by the late humorist Erma Bombeck, who said, "I would really like a gift that doesn't come with a warranty."

Alas, even when the intent is aesthetics, the result can fall short. One of my efforts being a case in point:

Even after our mother's death, our dad — dubbed Big Daddy by his grandchildren — dutifully attended whatever events his grown children and their families were involved in. But as the years passed, both his mobility and his interest in going anywhere beyond the bare necessities declined.

He was nearly 90 years old when he became homebound. About then, I accidentally became organist at a church in another county. Somehow, it just didn't seem right that Big Daddy was totally missing from that new chapter in my life.

One day while I was practicing for a wedding at the 'new' church, an idea dawned. The sanctuary was equipped with a for-then high tech recording setup. If Big Daddy couldn't come hear the music at this church, I'd take the music to him.

The long-suffering music director agreed to manipulate the recording equipment. So she with her book to read and me with my music to play got the program on tape.

That Saturday at Big Daddy's, I made sure his hearing aids were in, explained the 'treat' I'd brought for him, set up the machine by his recliner, and turned the volume up high enough to be sure he could hear the music.

While he listened, I went to the kitchen and busied myself with the usual Saturday food routine. Patting myself on the back for this brilliant idea did somewhat get in the way of unpacking groceries and cooking, but we both more or less settled in.

Or so I thought. About two-thirds of the way through the music, a woeful voice from the living room asked, "How long does this last?"

"About 30 minutes," I said. "Do you need a break?"

"No," Big Daddy replied. "I can take it."

That tape never even made it to a yard sale.

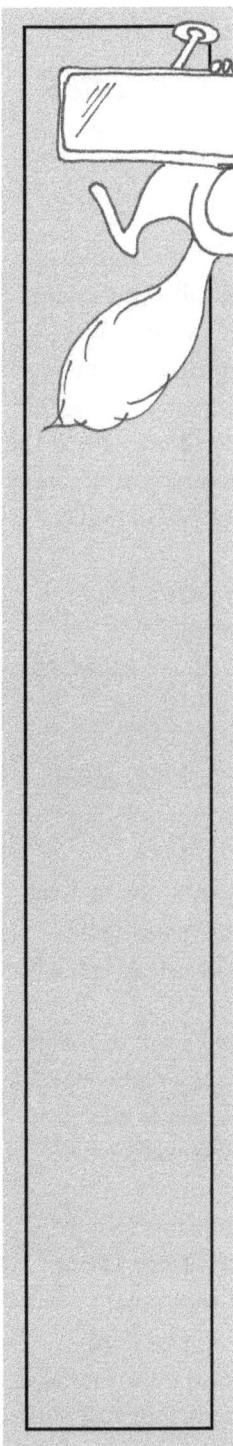

Predicaments

Stuffed-up Sinuses and Speaker Phones

After listening in on our call through no fault of their own,
the conferees were worried.

It's a relief to discover that our daughter Ellen in North Carolina is still speaking to me. Here's why: Yesterday, someone called me asking about a home remedy Ellen had recommended for stuffed-up sinuses. From our memories, the caller and I were able to somewhat patch together what the ingredients probably were.

I was okay with that till he said, "Close enough! I'll call my wife so she can fix a batch and start doctoring herself." After we hung up, it occurred to me that, in the interest of that wife's safety, I'd better get more specifics. So I called Ellen at her office.

The voice answering the phone didn't sound exactly right. "Ellen?" I asked. From a distance, I heard her say, "Mama, is that you?"

"Yes." She sounded like she was in a deep, hollow well so I added, "I can barely hear you."

"May I call you later when I'm at my desk?" she asked.

I thought about that poor patient using a remedy based on guesswork and said, "I need to talk to you now."

"Okay. But let me call you back."

In a couple of minutes, I got her call. It turns out that, in the first call, I misdialed Ellen's extension number and got the company's conference room. True to its name, the room was full of people, Ellen included, who were dutifully conferring.

After listening in on our call through no fault of their own, the conferees were worried. They suspended their business meeting long enough for Ellen to go to her desk and call me to find out what the crisis was.

Fortunately, once Ellen's co-workers heard that all was well give or take some stuffed-up sinuses, they had a good laugh.

Just in case someone else's sinuses are stopped up or plan to be, the recipe is: To a quart of distilled (very important detail) water, add one teaspoon of salt and one teaspoon of soda. Snort it up your nose.

But don't blame me if it doesn't work. I'll have to be pretty darn congested to try it. I'm just thankful that, mid-conference on the speaker phone, I didn't say something like, "Ellen, I need the recipe for that stuff to snort."

Small Acorns Cause Large Emergency

"I heard a rustle, rustle, swoosh in the woods just behind me. It was a grown black bear, coming down out of a tree about twenty yards away."

"Y ou sure picked a beautiful weekend to go hiking in the Smokies," I said.

"It's a hike I'll remember," Marcy replied, "because Deborah broke her leg."

First Presbyterian music director Marcy Lay had just returned from east Tennessee. Her time there had included an eight-mile hike on the Huskey Gap trail with her friend/hiking buddy/church organist Deborah Sanders.

Since the two are bird enthusiasts, they listened for the various songs and calls, and were somewhat disappointed that, by late afternoon, Marcy's repeated imitations of a barred owl call had not prompted a response from an owl.

On the last mile of the return trip, what they did hear off to their left was the piteous whimper of a bear cub up in a tree. They decided it was crying for its mama.

As dusk approached, they crossed a treacherous boulder field and started down a slope that supposedly was easier walking. Marcy turned to say something to Deborah and saw that she'd lost her footing and was hydroplaning on acorns. Rather than falling up the hill, Deborah fell forward and landed face down.

"Are you okay?" Marcy asked.

"No, I'm not," came the reply. "I heard something pop." When Deborah raised her head, the right side of her face was bloody and covered with imbedded leaves.

"About the time I saw all that blood," said Marcy, "I heard a rustle, rustle, swoosh in the woods just behind me. It was a grown black bear, coming down out of a tree about twenty yards away."

With Deborah sprawled on the ground, running was not an option. Marcy said, "I began to hit our trekking poles together over my head, scream like a crazy person, and lunge in the bear's direction flailing the poles."

The bear disappeared into the trees. Marcy wiped some of the leaves and blood off Deborah's face and tried to help her up. But Deborah couldn't put any weight on her right leg, and Marcy couldn't carry her.

"We could still hear the bear cub crying," said Marcy. "If its mama was still near the tree she'd come out of, we were between her and her cub. And when it comes to bears, that's about the worst place you can be."

With evening approaching, it began to look like Marcy would have to go the last half-mile of the trail alone to get help. But first, they tried the cell phone. Though it's seldom possible to get a signal along a hiking trail, the phone worked long enough for Deborah to call 911, which connected her to park rangers.

As they waited for the rangers, the barred owl they'd been hoping all day to hear started calling. And eventually the bear cub quit crying. They hoped its mama had circled around and found it. But they couldn't be sure the bear was gone.

"That was the longest 30 minutes of my life," Marcy said. She and Deborah began singing "How Firm a Foundation" and other hymns. Marcy recalled that, when she saw those rangers coming up the hill, "I was able to breathe again."

The rangers administered first aid and determined that additional help was needed. Deborah finished the hike strapped securely to a litter, staring at treetops in the fading daylight, borne by four Great Smokey Mountains National Park Search and Rescue team members.

In retrospect, Deborah and Marcy were grateful for several things: that the accident happened as near the end of the trail as it did; that they had gotten a rare phone connection; that help came before dark; and that the bear did not attack them. "We felt that God was with us."

The eventual diagnosis was two breaks in Deborah's leg — the tibia just above her hiking boot and the fibula below the knee. Both breaks are expected to heal without surgery, but she'll miss a few Sundays at the console.

As one church organist to another, I consoled Deborah by pointing out that both the tibia and fibula sound like they should be names for pipe organ stops.

Late the night of the accident, after a prolonged stay at the emergency room, the hikers finally reached the Sanders home. As Marcy and Deborah's husband Bill wheeled Deborah down the hallway in an office chair, she said, "Marcy…about you scaring the bear…that's a side of you I'd never seen before."

Meanwhile, somewhere in the deep dark woods of the Smokies, a mama bear soothed her cub with, "Dear, about the way that human was carrying on…sometimes there's just no explaining them."

Heroes Met, Lessons Learned While Melting a Mercury

The car had a full tank of gas. The back seat area was engulfed in flames that swirled round and round, roof to floorboard.

Did you know steel 'belts' in tires are actually wires not much bigger than those florists use to secure flowers in bouquets? I recently learned that the hard way.

I drove my dad (90 years old; a shrinking 6'4" frame; down probably 50 pounds from his healthier-days 270 norm; stubborn) to the barbershop in his '83 Mercury — a big, black luxury-type car. On the way back, it started bump-bumping like when a tire slowly goes flat.

We made it to his house, but when we stopped, smoke came out above the left front tire. Thick, ugly, stinky smoke. Getting out of a car for Big Daddy (family nickname), at this stage of life, is not speedy. The smoke kept getting worse. When he was finally standing, he said, "Pop that hood." He was gonna see if he could fix it!

After convincing him "no way," I fought the hard-to-unlock house door — by then, there were flames — and called 911. While I was in the house, the tire blew out and fire spread through the front of the car.

We got maybe 50 yards away and Big Daddy balked big time; didn't want to go beyond the apple tree shade. It wasn't far enough if the thing exploded, and the interior was now an inferno.

We snailed our way further. A car pulled over and asked if we needed help. I don't know our answer, but they decided 'yes.' The younger of the two men, sporting a tee shirt with some violent message on it, stayed beside us and chatted. The other one, after an emergency vehicle barreled by, stood on the roadside to flag down the next missile.

The two...let's call them gentlemen, since that's who they were... stayed with us until police/a fire truck arrived. As our two first-on-the-scene helpers left, I told the young man, "I even like your shirt."

The car had a full tank of gas. The back seat area was engulfed in flames that swirled round and round, roof to floorboard. When the fire truck arrived, I saw no way they could prevent an explosion that would make Hollywood jealous. I wanted them to be frantic like I'd been since seeing the first smoke. Instead, they calmly unrolled hoses, checked to insure there were no tangles, manned posts CLOSE TO THE CAR, as if they didn't know better, and began dousing the fire.

Afterwards, I insisted on looking. The tire where the fire started was a bouquet of tiny wires. The front was a crumbling charcoal skeleton; the steering wheel was melted, and those leather seats were showing their last layer of foam rubber. Groceries in the back seat floor area, including now 'char-broiled' lamb…well, go figure. Big Daddy's car had become a was. When they towed it off, a large puddle of disintegrated car guts spilled into the driveway.

One of those strange coincidences: an on-scene fireman had been getting a haircut while Big Daddy was. "I was just bragging at the barber shop about the mileage on my Mercury," Daddy reminded him. "I guess I'll have to change that tune."

Here are some things that went right. The policeman (a former student of mine), once he located us, did what was needed: he calmed us. Once the fire was out, he helped us back to the house, then got out of the way when he saw he could.

The firemen put the fire out. The one who was gathering data asked questions respectfully and answered ours in like manner.

Here are some lessons learned: If a door lock is nigh on to impossible to negotiate under normal circumstances, have it replaced. It can eat up urgent time in an emergency.

If a call to 911 gets disconnected by the frantic caller, they'll call back. (I don't know if this works with a cell phone.) 911 can get the address from a landline phone number, but it really is important to have a legible house address where it can be read from the road.

Know where your garden hose is. For heaven's sake, buy a fire extinguisher, read the directions, and keep it handy.

Worry about a sudden suspicious car noise, even if the dashboard lights are calm. If the noise gets worse, stop and check. Should you kinda think you might sort of smell smoke, home being less than a mile away is irrelevant. Now, it's the smell that haunts — appearing when it isn't really there.

In my opinion, several heroes earned a claim to fame during our Mercury melt: The ones wearing the uniforms earned that title by doing their jobs. And the ones out of uniform? That old 'don't judge a book by its cover' adage applies to 'don't judge heroes by their shirt messages' as well.

Two Turtledoves…and a Squirrel?… in a Pear Tree

No driver's manual had prepared G. S. for driving a car while
peering through the hind legs of a squirrel
swinging from the visor.

As pear tree owners know, before the fruit gets ripe enough to harvest, squirrels will eat it until the trees are bare. So keeping the little varmints at bay becomes a top priority.

One local gardener (we'll call her Joan) recently found herself in this very dilemma. As she gazed out the window, dreaming of pear preserves and mincemeat, what she saw was squirrels ready and waiting to feast in her pear tree.

Joan's Good Samaritan neighbor (herein known as G. S.) heard of her plight and offered to trap the pesky rodents.

Squirrel No. 1 was quite accommodating — took the bait and was hauled off to greener, pear-less pastures. So Joan's song of woe changed to a parody on *The Twelve Days of Christmas*:

> In the last week of Ju-une
> a neighbor trapped for me
> the squir-rels in my pear tree.

Squirrel No. 2 posed no problem as far as its trapping went. But a slight complication arose when G. S.'s dog (we'll call him Dawg) entered the picture. Dawg was used to going for rides with his master, and did not consider a caged squirrel reason enough for him to stay home. So he hopped into the back seat alongside the trap.

When Joan's dog (let's name him Dagwood) saw Dawg in the car, he begged to go along also. Softhearted G. S. gave in and added Dagwood to the back seat mix. Away he and his eclectic bunch of passengers went.

Dagwood gets the blame for somehow unfastening the cage door and freeing the squirrel. G. S.'s car was a spacious one, but its back seat could not accommodate a terrified squirrel being chased by two full-grown Labrador Retrievers. So the squirrel leapt into the front seat, followed of course by the two labs.

A squirrel running back and forth across the dashboard can diminish one's ability to drive safely. But G. S. had a delivery to make — more specifically, a critter to relocate — so on he went, trying to ignore the menagerie-gone-berserk. Suddenly the squirrel jumped down from the dashboard to the floorboard on the passenger side. There, Dagwood cornered and caught it.

"Turn that squirrel loose!" G. S. yelled, and Dagwood miraculously obeyed. The released squirrel immediately leapt for the nearest 'higher ground,' which turned out to be G. S.'s shoulder. With two barking labs hot on its heels, this perch wasn't high enough. So it climbed to a better perch — G. S.'s head.

Next, the squirrel leapt toward the visor, grabbed its edge and hung on with all its wee might. No driver's manual had prepared G. S. for driving a car while peering through the hind legs of a squirrel swinging from the visor. Yet somehow, he managed not only to steer, but also to lower the passenger-side window. And somehow, the squirrel took advantage of that escape route.

Back at his neighbor's tree, as G. S. reset the trap, he voiced two regrets. First, he was concerned that Squirrel No. 2 exited the car too near their neighborhood and might reappear in Joan's tree. Secondly, he said, "I wish someone had had a video camera."

In conclusion, a couple of messages:

To future squirrels captured from Joan's pear tree: rest assured that when you leave the neighborhood, you will be the sole passenger in the back seat of G. S.'s car.

To anyone who, due to a recent hallucination, decided to get psychoanalysis: you can cancel that appointment. You really did see a man driving down the road with a squirrel on his head.

Sporting Chance

A Farm Team's Summer of Trials and Victories

"Strike one!" the umpire would yell from behind the plate.
In the crowd, the pitcher's foster dad
would stand up and yell, "That's a quarter!"

In the summer of 1962, it fell my lot to help with a Little League farm team. My brother Donnie was the coach. He had an assistant, but they both had fulltime jobs. Plus, Donnie sometimes went straight from work to Nashville to rehearsals of the Peabody College outdoor theater production of Gilbert and Sullivan's *The Mikado*.

I was home for the summer, just rattling around, and began attending ball practice. On the rare occasions when neither real coach could be there, I'd be in charge. Part of this responsibility was picking up most of the players in our big green station wagon.

There was a practice field behind the Tennessee Knitting Mills building on South Main. When the station wagon doors opened at that destination, those ragtag little fellows took over that field. They took over the hearts of our family, too. Some of them often went home with us to spend the night. For the entire summer, their dramas became our dramas.

Midseason, the team suffered a setback when our practice field was literally pulled out from under us to become part of the road construction that is now Carmack Boulevard. Within a week, a parent who worked with heavy machinery converted our cow pasture into a practice field.

We weren't supposed to win games. But our fielders — even the one who was so little, the weight of his glove tipped him to the left — seldom missed a fly ball. Roger, our hind-catcher, gave new meaning to the word 'hustle.' And ask me if we had a pitcher.

"Strike one!" the umpire would yell from behind the plate.

In the crowd, the pitcher's foster dad would stand up and yell, "That's a quarter!" Raymond would grin a big goofy grin in his dad's direction, rare back, and throw another strike.

"That's another quarter!" rang from the stands, answered by another grin.

During games, the powers that be wouldn't let me in the dugout. I had to cheer us on, and join in the team's ack-ack-ack-ack-ack noise intimidation, literally hanging on the chain-link fence. It was the nearest I ever came to protesting for Women's Lib.

The week of Peabody's performance of *The Mikado*, I decided to invite the farm team. They all accepted. The night of that outing, one teenage helper and I began collecting team members. Soon, that station wagon was bulging at the seams with squirmy, giggling boys. Up front, one was under my elbow, another in Jane's lap. The back seat filled up and overflowed into the luggage space.

As we approached the last teammate's house, I called out, "Some of you might ought to duck down. Ted's mom may not let him go if she sees how crowded we are."

I pulled up to the curb and glanced around to see if anyone had ducked. Every one of them was doubled over, creating a panoramic view of little boy bottoms. They stayed that way until, with Ted in tow, we got out of sight of his house.

Our entourage took up most of a long row near Peabody's outdoor stage. My worries about crowd control were for naught. The boys were enthralled with the show. Their only 'disruptive' behavior came whenever any large male actor appeared onstage.

As if on cue, the entire row would rise, turn toward me, and ask in unison, "Is that Donnie?"

Meanwhile, back at the ball diamond, our team had become recognized as, to put it mildly, a contender. After winning close games, The Fountain, a drive-in a block beyond the hospital on Trotwood, was a favorite place to celebrate wins. Donnie, surrounded by a cloud of grimy-uniformed boys, ended so many games at — and sometimes in — The Fountain, our team placed first among the farm teams.

Ronnie, Roger, Raymond, Randy... All those little guys didn't have names that began with "r." But they all had spirit. On TV, I watch today's sweaty millionaire athletes mouth platitudes like "we played with heart." The players on that summer-of-'62 Dr. Pepper Farm Team could not have put it into words. But, in its purest form, "playing with heart" is what they did.

The Ups and Downs of 'Just for the Halibut' Fishing

When we finally stopped, the sensation was like being in a washing machine except uppy-down rather than side-to-side.

"You need to go halibut fishing, Mama," said Kate. "It's what people do when they come to Alaska."

Hence Kate, Ellen and I learned that Homer, Alaska, does not have a Hilton. Mostly, it has charter boats that leave early and go far to where the halibut are.

When a captain — let's call him Todd — strode into our gathering place clad head-to-toe in waterproof wear and said, "Follow me," I waved to daughters and did as I was told.

So did two men from Oregon and three from Arkansas.

We roared out of the harbor, hitting the high spots of waves that, even near shore, were so riled that Todd, who constantly communicated by radio with someone as to conditions 'at sea,' dared not venture as far out as his favorite fishing spots.

Nevertheless, for over two hours we sped atop watery oblivion. I toyed with taking one of the motion-sickness pills Ellen had armed me with. But this trip was too expensive to risk 'may cause drowsiness' medication.

The boat was small. We seven, in the cabin or on deck, were a crowd. Shouting back and forth, we got acquainted. The older of the Oregon twosome, who was less than a year beyond open-heart surgery, had landed a 150-pound halibut from that same boat the day before. The Arkansas three would be on this boat again the next day. I was the only one-day fisherperson.

When we finally stopped, the sensation was like being in a washing machine except uppy-down rather than side-to-side. Never mind the roiling; let the fishing begin.

The men lined themselves up around the back rail; I sat on a small platform to the side. Each time our boat dipped low, water threatened to slosh in. Todd ignored my request for a life jacket. I later realized there was no point wearing one. If anyone fell into those frigid waters, instant hypothermia would set in.

Gear consisted of a heavy pole; three-pound weight; cut-fish bait literally big enough to choke a horse; huge reel. Halibut live near the bottom; we let out lots of line.

Mid-deck was a large ice-filled bin for storing fish in. Todd just threw the smaller species in there. 'Keeper' halibut he dropped onto the deck and, using a big club, whapped them in the head. He took my first halibut — a mere 20-pounder — off the hook and threw it back.

Todd also threw back my dogfish (an 18-inch-long pointy-nosed shark that curled itself around the bait), and a larger-than-dinner-plate starfish. I got to keep an ugly sea bass, a salmon, and the next halibut, which was larger than that first 'wee' one.

Any time someone snagged a halibut, that action took center-stage. Even the smaller ones' fighting, amplified by the pull and tug of fierce ocean currents, became a muscle-ripping battle.

The goal of the day on charters is for all to catch their limit of big fish. This wasn't happening, so we moved farther out to rougher waters. Todd rigged up everyone else's poles, but not mine.

I enjoyed watching adorable little puffin birds as they bobbed peacefully in troughs between the frantic waves. But after several minutes of sitting idly as the guys snagged halibut, I asked, "Why am I not fishing?"

"These waters are so rough, you wouldn't be able to reel in the bait and weight, much less a halibut," Todd explained. The venture's dollar amount swam before my eyes. "I think I want to try," I said.

The 30-plus-pounder in Ellen's freezer probably wishes Todd had ignored my request. But after wrestling it, when the next big one hit, I said, "Who wants this fish? It's yours for the reeling." It landed in a freezer somewhere in Arkansas.

The largest halibut of our catch was a mere 50 pounds. Its floundering (pardon the pun) on deck could have broken someone's bones. So as soon as it appeared under the water's surface, Todd pulled out a pistol and shot it dead.

When we finally had enough fish, Todd scurried graceful as a cat across the boat's bow, securing ropes and equipment. For an eternity, the motor's full-throttle roar, punctuated with resounding whaps as the boat belly-flopped across the angry ocean's surface, hinted that each breath might be our last.

Twelve hours after departure, we reached our harbor. And before our feet touched the ground, this one-day fisherperson was dreaming of someday going again.

Our Mother, the Sit-Com Bowler

Her right hand, which held the ball, eased down beside her. The whole idea seemed to be, "If I can just get rid of this thing, maybe no one will notice I had it in the first place."

The new minister of our parents' church came into the pulpit with the Bible in one hand, a songbook in the other, and a determination that God wants his people to live full, well-rounded lives.

When 'Brother Ben' found out how many Just Housewives were in his flock, he decided they needed recreation as an outlet. His expertise was bowling. Before the last handshake on his first Sunday, a bewildered bunch of beginners had signed up for his Housewives' League.

Mama was one of the signers. Not because she wanted to bowl, but because she always went to bat for the underdog. And Brother Ben, with his mission to, via bowling, bring true happiness to a bunch of mostly already happy housewives, was a definite underdog.

The league didn't last long, which did bring happiness to the dropouts. Except for Ben's long-suffering wife, Mama was the last to go. Long after the desertions, she feigned an interest just to help Ben save face.

Eventually, that feigned interest drew our family in. Though as adults we siblings had gone our separate ways, it occasionally fell our lot to Do Something Together. Perhaps as a subconscious effort to salvage some usefulness from all those Housewives' League hours, Mama suggested we all go bowling.

Buddy and Alice, who bowled regularly in a competitive league, got to designate team members. They headed up one team, balancing their skills on the opposing side with: Daddy, who had bowled in his youth; Don, who said he knew how; Don's wife Kathy, who took bowling in P.E. and hated it; and Mama, who knew where the concession stand and restrooms were. The rest of us were distributed at random. Both teams had the same number of people.

Buddy and Alice went first. They looked good. More importantly, when they finished with the choreography and turned themselves into statues, the ball rolled slightly off-center all the way down and knocked over a lot of pins.

With Daddy's first roll, we all realized that his bowling skills were not rusty. His feet hurt too much for gracefulness, but all the pins fell the first time. And the second.

Mama was next. With a bowling ball clutched to her midriff, she sort of accidentally emerged from the crowd that was congratulating Daddy. Her right hand, which held the ball, eased down beside her. The whole idea seemed to be, "If I can just get rid of this thing, maybe no one will notice I had it in the first place."

A few more mincing, duck-walk steps and she was at the line. She dropped the ball. It bounced, then ambled its weaving way down the alley. Buddy came up and gently began explaining technique. After a few words, his advice was drowned out by falling pins. Mama's strike got added to Daddy's two.

The evening's die was cast. Whenever it was Mama's turn, she would glance around to see if anyone was noticing, turn loose of the offending ball, and as it made its 'drunken sailor' way down the lane, sidle off toward some other batch of bowlers. Once, she got so embarrassed she just lowered the ball into the gutter. That set our team back. But we soon convinced her she was doing good. She rallied, and so did our leading edge.

By the end of the game, Daddy's dusted off skills combined with Mama's inept accuracy had not only overcome the rest of our team's lack of talent. It had bested Alice and Buddy's near-professional know-how.

We won. As far as I know, Mama and Daddy never bowled again. And I'm certain that bowling was never again our family's 'Do Something Together' destination.

Current 'Orange Madness' and Former Basketball Glory

Once the buzzer sounds, we agonize when players who could previously do no wrong suddenly become bumbling caricatures of their former capable selves.

Soon after last Sunday's service was over, I tracked down a church member with the sole intent of teasing her about her decidedly orange jacket. She wears it whenever University of Tennessee teams pull off some extra special victory. Her wardrobe this Sunday was celebrating wins by both the men's and women's basketball teams. The Big Orange men's win advanced them to NCAA's March Madness Sweet Sixteen.

"This may be my last chance to wear it this year," my orange-blooded friend added wistfully.

Standing nearby was a man whose brother was conspicuous by his absence. I asked if recent health problems had recurred. "He's probably just mourning the fact that Vanderbilt lost," was the answer. "He's as big a Vandy fan as (pointing to the orange jacket) she is UT."

Thus it goes this time of year. As the nation's best teams rise to the top, then topple till one team is declared champion, armchair athletes universally cheer victories or share the pain of their team's defeat. For those of us on the home front, Mondays through Wednesdays are pointless days to merely endure. On Thursdays, it's game time!

Once the buzzer sounds, we agonize when players who could previously do no wrong suddenly become bumbling caricatures of their former capable selves. That's when, in front of our TV set, Jesse waxes reminiscent. Missed free throws...careless passes that result in turnovers...failed transitions from defense to the other end of the court...all remind him of practice strategies he witnessed in his youth.

If a free throw fails, he recalls: "Every day when practice was over, 'our' boys had to make 20 free throws in a row before going to the locker room. They got really good at making free throws."

An errant pass brings to mind a low-tech strategy that resulted in accurate ball handling: "Coach DeShazo would take a regulation basketball, cut it in two, stuff it with rags, and sew it back up. Then he'd have the players stand in a big circle and pass that heavy ball really fast to each other."

The team eventually became adept at catching and throwing the rag-filled ball. In comparison, handling the air-filled variety was a breeze.

As to transition from their rival's end of the court? DeShazo assigned two players designated spots on the floor of their own court. "When the opponent shoots the ball, you go there and you be there!" he told them. Whoever rebounded the ball was to throw it immediately, not to a person, but to one of those two spots.

In 1949, as statistician for the Humboldt High School boys' basketball team, Jesse had firsthand knowledge of these and other practice strategies. That's the year Humboldt, with a 44-0 undefeated season, became Tennessee's state champion.

Jesse remembers that, although many of Humboldt's games were easy wins, they did have some challenges. One of those came when Coach DeShazo was hospitalized. The team played a lackadaisical first half and went into the locker room on the short end of the score.

Coach's stand-in walked into that locker room, silently surveyed the dejected players, and said, "You all must've forgotten to bring your press clippings. These boys just don't know how good you are!" Then he turned on his heel and walked out. The game ended with a lopsided victory for Humboldt.

Of course, along with coaching know-how, the Humboldt team had more than its share of raw talent. One of its first stringers was Doug Atkins, who rose to hall-of-fame stature as an NFL football player.

That was then, this is now. Schools now compete according to size of enrollment rather than across-the-board. And college teams are once again embroiled in end-of-year competition.

By today's church service, most of us will already know whether UT is still in the March Madness fray. For those who don't follow the games, all the update you'll need will be the presence — or absence — of that orange jacket in the pews.

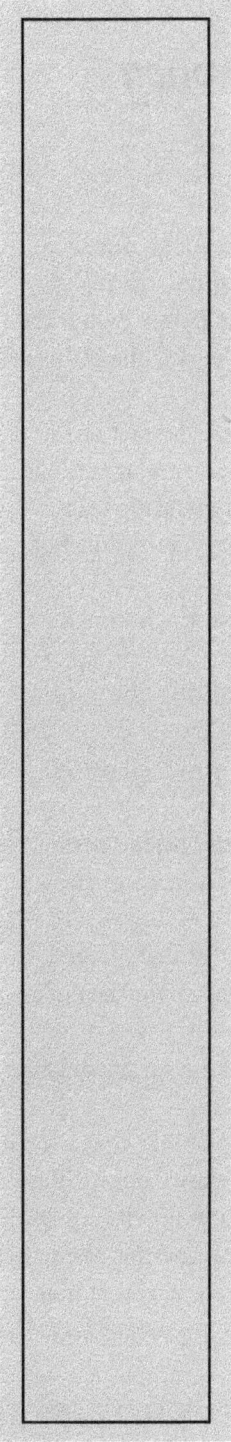

Et Cetera

Cashing in a Long-Lost Policy

If that policy had been important enough to sell,
it should be important enough to close out now.

$126.45 — a check made out to me. Two impersonal signatures are stamped on it by an insurance company. But I know better. The real signature is my mother's, hastily scribbled over forty years before, when she agreed to pay ten cents a week for twenty full years. She was the insured, I the beneficiary.

Two years after her death, I found the policy in a safe deposit box and showed it to banker Waymon Hickman, knowing it wasn't worth much. We sat in the urgently plush office, talking business, pretending tears weren't plopping into my lap. He verified the policy's meager value, but encouraged me to cash it in.

For several months, the policy laid around the house. Each time I straightened, it got tucked into another obscure corner. One extra penniless straightening day when I found it in a heap of to-do's, the paper work I so dreaded began to take form and shape:

January — I wrote a letter to the insurance company named on the policy.

February — A pleasant letter arrived from a company three states from where my letter had been sent. They needed a photocopy of the policy's first page.

Since the word 'amicable' was part of their name, I was encouraged. With intentions of dealing with this immediately, I laid down the envelope.

March — During another housecleaning, the envelope surfaced. I sent off the requested copy.

April 15 — A letter arrived from 'the amicables' explaining that twelve years previously they "sold this business to various insurance companies." Included were addresses of three companies that might have the policy.

The affable ending to the letter seemed sour to me. I resented the parent company shuttling the detective work back to the customer. If that policy had been important enough to sell, it should be important enough to close out now.

I called a local insurer to see if my judgment was too harsh. He said this type run-around by others made his job difficult; he suggested I take my problem to the state Department of Insurance. The envelope and the decision were laid aside for a few days, deliberately this time.

April 25 — I decided to give the company one more chance by writing the person who had corresponded with me thus far.

May — A different name was signed to the short letter saying their company would do no more. Since going to the Department of Insurance would probably begin yet another drawn-out ordeal, I deliberated some more.

June — A simple business letter with the necessary information was sent to all three addresses in the April 15 letter. If this fizzled, I would take my local insurer's advice.

July — Two negative replies came in quick succession.

August — The third company sent a crude memo-size form with a couple of checkmarks in blanks. In furry type, the amount of $126.45 was sloppily stamped at the bottom. They had the policy, but wanted me to send in the original. I did, immediately (keeping a copy).

September 26 — I am $126.45 richer. This tiny legacy from the past qualifies as hard-earned money. How nice if it would last as long as the scattered efforts to retrieve it. Now, what to do with it to honor its intent?

It lands in an account that pays for music lessons, veterinary bills, and other basic extras. Across the years, I sense the merest nod of approval.

Biblical Ecological Activists

"Thou beast!" one of the women screeched.
"How darest thou give yon big fish a tummyache?"

According to my calendar, Earth Day is near. I both practice and applaud efforts to be considerate of the flora and fauna we share our planet with. But one wonders how current sensitivities might have affected events in Biblical times.

Could environmental awareness have divided the ranks of Noah's family? There they were, afloat in an overcrowded boat, up to their elbows in orangutans. And with no land in sight, what they smelled was not the roses.

One son started shoveling elephant poop overboard. "For shame, Shem!" scolded his brother. "Thou hast fouled the waters for the fishes. How would you like it if someone shoveled waste into thy dwelling place?"

"That art the whole point, Ham," grumbled Shem. "It's already here." He turned to his other brother for support. "Dost thou agree?"

"Yeth," said Japheth. Shem handed Japheth a shovel and told Ham, "Thou should either help, or go elsewhere to sulk."

About then the wind shifted, coming straight from the pigpen. Ham picked up a shovel and got busy. He was so enthusiastic, he on-the-spot invented the 'work song' by leading the trio in some rollicking Gregorian chants.

While we're still in deep water, let's see how Jonah would have fared in the company of animal rights activists: After a long, uncomfortable time in the belly of the fish, Jonah found himself spit out. Instead of drowning, he'd washed up belly-down on a sandy shore. He eased one eye open. The first thing he saw was — toes. Three sets of them, each with different-colored nail polish.

"Thou beast!" one of the women screeched. "How darest thou give yon big fish a tummyache?"

Weak, disoriented, and half conscious, Jonah groaned, "I thought I was a goner."

"Humans," a prim voice said, "art not listed on the preferred diet for big fishes. Having a human wander your innards wouldn't have been a picnic for the fish, either."

"Girls," said the third woman, "thinketh thou that we three can haul him in for judgment day?"

"But," Jonah weakly protested, "I'm innocent! The fish swallowed *me* and…"

The women pulled Jonah to his feet, drug him to the town jail, and charged him with animal cruelty. On his day in court his plea to go to Nineveh never stood a chance. History as we know it never happened since poor Jonah rotted in jail, pining for the good old days in the fish's smelly belly.

Farther along, imagine what would be missing in the Old Testament had the era's Protectors of the Natural Order of Things gotten into this picture:

"I saw it with mine own eyes," one Protector vowed to another. "Though he be a mere slip of a boy, he sleweth the wolf with one stone. What's more, I hear he doth this deed often and braggeth about it to his brethren."

"Lo, though," a friend of David's family said, "he *is* a shepherd…and 'twas piteous bleats that hied him to the site…and the wolf *did* have a leg of lamb in its jaws…and David's job *is* to…"

"What hath this younger generation come to," interrupted the Protector, "that one amongst them hast senselessly slain a natural predator!"

An ordinance to confiscate David's slingshot failed solely because a large number of his kin were on the County Commission. Hence, not only did the area's wolf nose-count continue to diminish; also, the failed legislation sealed Goliath's eventual fate.

Then there's the battle of Jericho. Imagine how dramatically that outcome would have been altered by a noise ordinance.

Enough of past possibilities. Here in this century, it's time to go recycle something.

Theme and Variations on 'The Friendly Wave'

Friendly waves are a form of body language that don't get a lot of press.
Yet, in one form or another they play significant roles in our lives.

Each Sunday morning, an elderly man sits in a straight chair beside the front door to a roadside church in Stiversville. He is there to wave. As a car passes, his left arm creates two right angles — one at the shoulder, one at the elbow. He turns his open hand back and forth, back and forth. It is his signature wave.

I, for one, look forward to his greeting, expect it, and am let down when he's not there.

Eklutna, Alaska is on the four-lane divided highway between Fairbanks and Anchorage. On a rise near the western exit ramp at Eklutna are a couple of dilapidated couches — the kind that normally are set out by the roadside for disposal.

Almost any time of day, during the summer at least, townsmen from Eklutna sit on these couches and wave at passersby. The couches and the greetings have enhanced, perhaps even become, the town's identity.

Friendly waves are a form of body language that don't get a lot of press. Yet, in one form or another, they play significant roles in our lives. One type wave simply acknowledges others' presence. Politicians and beauty queens use these to advantage along parade routes. Their continuous waving may give them cramps; but, hey, the crowds expect these signs of acknowledgement.

A great favorite of mine in this category is the 'road' wave I grew up with. We'd be driving down some narrow country dirt road. To greet the driver of the occasional car we met, Daddy would lift his forefinger from the steering wheel and nod. He'd get some similar low-key but adequate response. If the other driver was someone he knew, the entire hand sometimes left the wheel. To not wave at every passing driver was the height of rudeness.

The 'goodbye' wave is a biggie. Doting parents encourage these waves by urging offspring to "wave 'bye to grandma." A baby's open-close version may be its first deliberate connection with other humans. On the first day of school or camp, a goodbye wave to parents by that same child can be filled with pathos and fear.

Ever since the movie industry began, it has turned goodbye waves into tear-jerkers. For years, cameras have zeroed in on friends, relatives, lovers weeping as they wave to passengers on a ship that's leaving shore, a bus disappearing down the highway, the speck of a window in a distant departing airplane.

At the other end of the spectrum, a wave of recognition in a crowded airport or bus or train station can create a huge sense of relief. Not only has the passenger arrived safely, but someone is there to meet them.

And who hasn't smiled at the contagious enthusiasm of a teenager's effervescent waving to friends just spotted in a crowd? Then there's the wave of encouragement, which can become a culprit if Junior is waving back to Dad in the bleachers instead of catching a pop-up fly.

'The wave' at sporting events is a meticulously orchestrated miracle. Hundreds of people stand and sit at the precisely necessary time to create humanity's version of an ocean wave. The whole point of this production is to show support/approval/encouragement to their team. In our age of worshipping ultimates, this may be the ultimate wave.

There was a month this summer when the Stiversville greeter wasn't there, and I worried; rejoiced at his return. Now, cold weather has kicked in and his wordless "Hello, how are you?" is gone for a while. But its friendly spirit lives on, be it on 31 South in Tennessee or half a world away in Eklutna, AK.

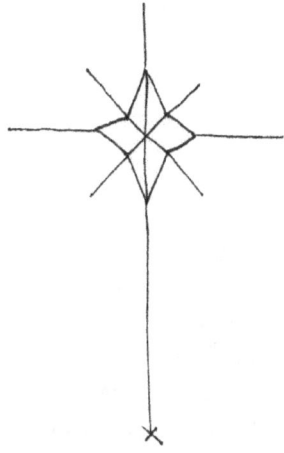

Meditations

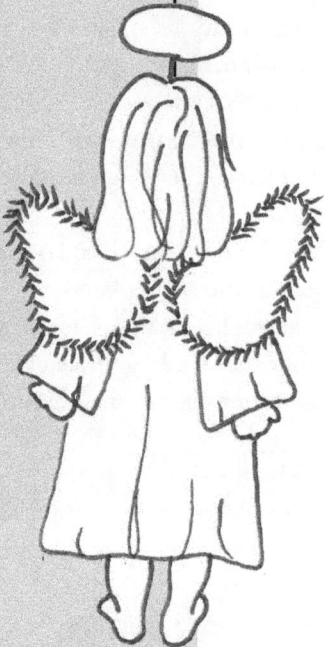

The Wooden Indian

*The soldier's workmanship denotes a talent the
mass-produced bears hadn't prepared me for.*

At the first hint of autumn, two of my friends dust off their addiction to craft fairs. Occasionally I join them on one of their many excursions. Today, their excitement is contagious as we wait in line to enter a fair known for its talented exhibitors.

Once inside the enormous, bustling hall, each of us is bent on seeing every shuck doll and calico bonnet. We soon drift apart. I amble from booth to booth, enjoying polished stones, woven baskets, the smell of leather, the tentative sound of folk instruments. Onlookers are clotted around a glass blower; also, at a potter's wheel. I admire items on the fringe of each display.

In the next booth, voices politely question an exhibitor. The carver — a middle-aged Indian — is tall, muscular, bronze; all Hollywood could ask for in a stereotype. His jeans and plaid shirt imply that buckskins would be an overstatement.

Amid the carving equipment, wooden bears in various stages of completion surround him. Obviously they are his main product. But deer, totem poles, and other standards crowd the booth's floor space. On dusty makeshift shelves at the back of the booth, a few more samples of this craftsman's work are displayed. One is a helmeted soldier — judging from the outfit, a foot soldier.

The soldier's workmanship denotes a talent the mass-produced bears hadn't prepared me for. His shoulders are bent as the strong bend, to lighten a load. War things bulge and dangle about his khakis. One hard-toed army boot indents the dirt road; the other shows a large hole. A strong hand with long, fine fingers reaches toward reunion; the eyes are joyful. He seems about to break into a run.

The young Indian face, though brightened by the sight of home, invites searching. "Ancestry be damned," it says. "Look at me and know what I have known...far lands and habits, so unreal to you here, I may not speak and you not ask. But that it happened, you must agree."

People are gathered around the craftsman, listening to his light banter.

Asking questions, learning of bears. My back is to them. But if I cry for no reason among the carvings, it will be embarrassing. I walk off without looking back.

Other displays have lost their appeal. A need to better know the secrets of the wooden soldier swings me around the display hall and back to my spot at its feet. A man comes and looks. He reaches for the soldier, finds it glued down. He makes an impatient gesture, then turns away.

The Indian's admirers have drifted off. He comes toward me, a hospitable clerk amid the bears.

"The soldier statue is lovely," I say.

"Thank you." He is affable but guarded.

"I think I know three things about it." Our glances cross, then avoid each other. "Will you tell me if I'm right?"

"Certainly."

"It took you a long time to carve it."

"You're right so far," he answers. I sense his indulgent smile.

I whisper. "You love it very much."

He reels back as from a blow, and nods. Staring at the statue, I blurt, "And it's not for sale."

"If I charged by the hour, no one could buy it." He leaves abruptly, not offering a bear, and stands apart from me in his allotted booth space.

Why is he so disturbed that I have seen his soul? It's there in plain sight. In every knife-move of the son/brother/friend he fashioned. The wooden replica has captured one moment — that first reunion after the War — as surely as with a camera lens.

I want the soldier to tell me: Why did before-the-war closeness evaporate? What severed the bonds between sculpted and sculptor? Have you died, or does your carver simply deny that you exist? In the statue you still live...fresh, full of hope. Dusty.

As for your carver? What a strong warrior against despair he is. He enjoys his bears, and the admiring crowds. He sits just so, straight-backed, a practiced inscrutable look cocooning him while he works. But he won't allow that look while chatting with customers. Aloofness doesn't sell bears.

And the soldier is not for sale.

The Good Friday Possum

"It seems cruel," someone says, "but it's the sensible solution."

A traffic jam has made me late for our Good Friday service —
for me, the most meaningful worship experience of the Christian year.
Rather than interrupt with a late entrance, I just won't go. I might as well
pick up groceries while I'm out.

A fine misty rain smears my windshield as I turn in at the shopping
center. Something is out of kilter in the parking lot; what, I don't know.
But I'm grateful for a large, vacant section in front of the grocery.

That's it! That's what's wrong — the best parking spots are empty, on a
Friday, with rain beginning to fall. I steer toward the empty area.

An object — some small animal — is on the deserted pavement. My
car eases nearer. Through a peephole hastily wiped in the fogged window,
I see a bedraggled gray possum sitting on its haunches, its head bowed
to the right. Slow drops of blood seep down the pointed nose. Its mouth
gapes open, silhouetting precise rows of tiny sharp teeth. The eyes are
beginning to glaze.

Nothing, no one is near. The animal's agony seems to suspend it alone
in time and space.

Noise from the grocery gets my attention. The manager, a policeman,
and two employees are huddled at the entrance, talking and gesturing
toward the possum and me. They want me to move, so I park a good distance away, tie on a rain scarf, and hurry toward the store. Customers are
milling around outside the store, gawking at the possum.

"What happened?" I ask.

"Just a possum in the parking lot," someone mumbles. "Folks got to
complaining, so they called the law to get rid of it."

"Was it run over?" I ask the policeman.

"No'm." He almost smiles. "It was just ambling around when I got
here. Didn't have no cage with me, and couldn't shoot it — the bullet
might richochet. Had to hit it with my nightstick."

"It's still alive."

"Yes'm. It'll die soon. But they're dangerous, wounded like that. I'll
come back and take it off." The weathered, rugged face shows neither
regret nor enjoyment.

The manager is a different story. His usual calm has given way to nervous glances that flit between departing customers and people gazing out the plate glass window. His hands pleat and unpleat the sides of his butcher's apron.

"It seems cruel," someone says, "but it's the sensible solution."

I hurry into the store and wrench a cart from the line of empty ones. Somewhere between the pickles and the soup, wispy thoughts begin. 'Alone and dying...' Better concentrate on cereal.   '...the crowd afar off, watching...' Maybe I should just leave. '...important people upset; the sensible solution...'

Any other day — any other Friday — these peculiar ideas wouldn't envelope me like the misty rain that is soaking everything outside. I write a check with the same mechanical precision as the automatic door that opens to let me out. On the way to the car, I involuntarily glance at the possum. It is still alive, but now mutely sways from side to side. Dark drops of blood continue to fall from the tip of its nose, slowly widening the crimson puddle on the pavement beside it.

I hurry by, put my groceries in the trunk, slam the lid shut, drive off. Halfway to the street, I circle back to the possum magnet.

I have returned to stare; to absorb the suffering; to deliberately parallel this bleeding, dying creature's condition with Christ's crucifixion.

The possum's eyes no longer focus, but reflect pain beyond terror. '... as Christ's pain-glazed eyes fight for consciousness, did the women of Jerusalem hurry home from fishmongers' stalls, their shopping cut short by a sky mysteriously darkened?'

The possum's gaping mouth conveys total resignation. '...a gaping mouth struggles with "I am athirst"...' Not smoothly stated with a clear eye toward posterity.

The steady sway of the drenched possum settles into the pulse of eternity's sorrow. '...drops of blood, falling from a crown of thorns, create a splattery metronome at the foot of a cross...'

Both dyings are real. Isolated. Slow.

The manager comes out of the grocery, hesitant, trying to decide whether to again shoo me away. I leave, not looking back, no longer ashamed of my thoughts. Misty rain or not, I now see clearly what wondrous love is this; and, through this mute, dying possum, have worshipped on Good Friday.

Gladys' Christmas Song

She never got down to business voice-wise; just kept it quiet and simple.
Then it was gone.

Gladys Allen was a big woman. And her skin was the richest, warmest brown of all the shades ever passed out. She must've been in her late 50s when we first met. Her church and the one where I was organist were planning a service together, and Gladys was to sing a solo. Her sister brought her to my house so we could practice.

Gladys was ill at ease, partly because of me being white (it was that era), and partly due to her innate shyness. The three of us chatted several minutes before she relaxed. "We'd better practice," I finally said.

God bless America, what a voice! It was equal to watching ocean waves or waking to mist in the mountains or hearing snow whisper in the trees. All that wonder wrapped up in this quiet cook and housekeeper.

The day of the church service, Gladys was like a kid in a school play. She kept opening the heavy door to the sanctuary just enough to see who was in the pews. It was bothering her, too.

"I've worked for most of the folks out there," she fretted.

"Don't you worry about that," I answered. "You just get up there and sing."

She did. They heard, and shared the wonder.

After that, our paths didn't cross very often. She owned a coffee shop that kept her busy, and my schedule stayed hectic. But we both belonged to a community chorus. Whenever the group sang for spring pilgrimages or caroled at Christmas, Gladys and I would catch up on our visiting. And I'd get to hear her sing.

Even after an operation on her throat just about cut her voice in half, Gladys was spellbinding on the spirituals. But each time I saw her, she seemed smaller, and weaker.

That last Christmas, we caroled from the balcony of the county's oldest church, where breathing the air gets you dizzy with tradition. After the program, we were riding back to town with friends.

"Gladys, there's an old song I've always wanted you to sing for me." I named it. "Will you sing it, here and now? Please?"

An embarrassed silence settled in the car before the shadows of her voice began "Precious Lord, Take My Hand." She never got down to business voice-wise; just kept it quiet and simple. Then it was gone.

Now, so is she. Having a high time singing with the heavenly host.

But about this time every year, Gladys closes the book of Glorias and Hallelujahs. Everything gets quiet; the hosts of angels settle down to listen.

Then, Gladys looks down for certain folk on earth — those whose old heartaches are haunting them at Christmas; those with terrible fresh hurts too heavy; those in pain and those beyond. Right in the middle of all those carols, Gladys sings on their behalf:

> *Precious Lord, take my hand,*
> *Lead me on, let me stand,*
> *I am tired, I am weak, I am worn;*
> *Through the storm, through the night,*
> *Lead me on to the light,*
> *Take my hand, precious Lord,*
> *Lead me home.*

Simple and soft it sounds, like when she sang it for me.

After the words are over, she keeps humming the tune: of a sudden, all the tears from human eyes swoop up to the heavens, where they gather to form a sparkling star. And beneath that star, an infant's tiny hand takes hold of a mother's finger, real personal-like.

Somehow, the strength in that tiny grip heaves humanity out of that old sloe of despondency. Hollowness isn't healed, but it's helped. And that's the best Hallelujah of them all.

Thank you, Gladys Allen. But I still miss you down here at Christmas.

Comparing the Processes That
Create Music and Sonnets

Practicing/playing music has a directness that can't be avoided…
Getting the job done with writing is another case altogether.

I recently read *Bird by Bird*, Anne Lamott's craft book about writing. Therein, Lamott states that her goal as a writer is to put on paper the things her characters have to say.

As someone who spends considerable time in two worlds — music and writing — this perspective made me wonder about what similarities, and differences, exist in the creation of music and writings.

Just as Lamott tries to stay out of her characters' way, I, as a church organist, hope to get out of the way and become a vessel through which music flows from its composer to current listeners. The route to accomplishing this goal is, sigh, practice.

If the music has inherent value, polishing it is a step toward sharing that value with receptive ears. The reality being, that goal's loftiness seldom happens during the actual presentation of music. Playing for a church service is a mish-mash of physical and mental calisthenics: getting cues (is that the minister's final word, or will cranking up the hymn cut into the next sentence; can I mirror the precise tempo the director is setting, etc.); coordination (changing stops, turning pages, not falling off the bench); and dealing with the always-waiting-in-the-wings nervousness.

Despite all this, the end result sometimes sounds like music.

Arriving at that point is very different from 'finishing' a manuscript. With music, the thing has boundaries from some other brain. Perhaps an editor has superimposed his or her markings, and the person performing the composition may add interpretation. But the result has a beginning, middle, and end that are solidly the composer's.

With writing, the outcome is indeterminate. Getting from rough draft to polished manuscript is fraught with pitfalls. What seemed solid in the mind's eye can lose shape and form en route from the brain to the fingertips. A lot of definitive writing is, I think, embedded in my elbows.

It's easier to know you're right (or wrong) in music. If I've played a piece of music as good as I can get it, it's probably during a practice session when no one is in hearing range. But on rare occasions when every word, every comma in a writing seems as perfected as time, effort, and know-how can make it, that writing stays 'right' long enough to share.

Practicing/playing music has a directness that can't be avoided. You sit down, open the music, and get on with it. Getting the job done with writing is another case altogether. Avoidance skills are often honed to a fine art; the only time I know how many splinters are in my hands is when I'm trying to write.

Both music and writing are genres where centuries of excellence inspire, challenge, and can overwhelm us. Yet we might as well jump in and do our dab, and do it as best we can. That dab just may have value and interest for someone somewhere along the way.

Acknowledgements

I am immensely indebted to my children:

Walt, who listened when I said I'd be interested in a graduate writing program and sent information about the one at Vermont College...

Ellen, who in her high school years illustrated columns, and has revived that skill for this collection...

Kate, whose patience and expertise have made it possible to wade through the murky waters of publication;

and to *The Daily Herald* newspaper in Columbia, Tennessee, for publishing my weekly Somewhere Along the Way column for lo these many years.